THE
RESURRECTION OF CHRIST

"Dr. Ramsey's book is a valuable study of what the Resurrection means for genuine Christianity."   THE OBSERVER

"Its sane grasp of the truth of the doctrine of the Resurrection should commend it to clergy and laity alike."
CHURCH TIMES

"No one can study this admirable little book without realising, better than before, the place of the Resurrection in Christian life and thought."
BIRMINGHAM POST

"This constructive study in Biblical theology can be warmly recommended to all students and teachers: while the general reader will find in it much to enjoy."
THE CHURCH OF ENGLAND NEWSPAPER

Religious Books in the Fontana Series

The Resurrection of Christ

A STUDY OF THE EVENT AND ITS MEANING
FOR THE CHRISTIAN FAITH

MICHAEL RAMSEY
Archbishop of York

COLLINS
fontana books

Contents

CHAPTER I

The Resurrection and the New Testament

I

THE WRITER of this book remembers receiving something of a shock when it was first his privilege to attend the lectures of the late Sir Edwyn Hoskyns. The lecturer began with the declaration that as our subject was the Theology and Ethics of the New Testament we must begin with the passages about the Resurrection. It seemed to contradict all the obvious preconceptions. Was it not right to trace first the beginnings of the ministry of Jesus, the events of His life and the words of His teaching? Here, surely, the essence of the Gospel might be found, and as a finale the Resurrection comes so as to seal and confirm the message. No. The Resurrection is a true starting-place for the study of the making and the meaning of the New Testament.

We are tempted to believe that, although the Resurrection may be the climax of the Gospel, there is yet a Gospel that stands upon its own feet and may be understood and appreciated before we pass on to the Resurrection. The first disciples did not find it so. For them the Gospel without the Resurrection was not merely a Gospel without its final chapter: it was not a Gospel at all. Jesus Christ had, it is true, taught and done great things: but He did not allow the disciples to rest in these things. He led them on to paradox, perplexity and darkness; and there He left them. There too they would have remained, had He not been raised from death. But His Resurrection threw its own light backwards upon the death and the ministry that went before; it illuminated the paradoxes and disclosed the unity of His words and deeds. As Scott Holland said: " In the Resurrection it was not only the Lord who was raised from the dead, His life on earth rose with Him; it was lifted up into its real light " (On Behalf of Belief, p. 12).

9

It is a desperate procedure to try and build a Christian Gospel upon the words of Jesus in Galilee apart from the climax of Calvary, Easter and Pentecost. If we do so we are professing to know Jesus better than the first disciples knew Him; and the Marcan record shews us how complete was their perplexity before the Resurrection gave them the key. Every oral tradition about Jesus was handed down, every written record of Him was made only by those who already acknowledged Him as Lord, risen from the dead.

It is therefore both historically and theologically necessary to " begin with the Resurrection." For from it, in direct order of historical fact, there came Christian preaching, Christian worship, Christian belief. Of the preaching much will be said in the pages that follow. As to the worship, the most stupendous change followed the Resurrection : Hebrew monotheists, without forsaking their monotheism, worshipped Jesus as Lord. As to the belief, there meets us throughout the Apostolic writings a close connection between the Resurrection and the Christian belief in God. The God of the Christians is essentially the God who raised Jesus Christ from the dead. In Paul's words they " believe on him that raised Jesus our Lord from the dead " (Rom. iv. 24). In Peter's words they are " believers in God, which raised him from the dead and gave him glory; so that your faith and hope might be in God " (1 Peter i. 21). Christian theism is Resurrection-theism. Similarly Christian ethics are Resurrection ethics, defined and made possible by men being " raised together with Christ " (Col. iii. 1). What is perhaps the earliest known Christian hymn contains the words

" Awake, thou that sleepest, and arise from the dead, and Christ shall shine upon thee." (Eph. v. 14.)

II

The Gospel of God appears in Galilee : but in the end it is clear that Calvary and the Resurrection are its centre. For Jesus Christ came not only to preach a Gospel but to *be* a

Gospel, and He is the Gospel of God in all that He did for the deliverance of mankind.

The Greek word "evangelion," that lies behind the word "gospel" in our English versions, is very rare; and its meaning in the New Testament is apparent only when we turn to the Old Testament, where the corresponding verb is specially used for God's coming intervention to deliver His people. The word tells of the good news that God is come, bringing (to use the Biblical words) salvation, righteousness, remission of sins, peace, mercy. "O thou that tellest good tidings to Zion, get thee up into the high mountain; O thou that tellest good tidings to Jerusalem, lift up thy voice with strength; lift it up, be not afraid; say unto the cities of Judah, Behold your God! Behold, the Lord GOD will come as a mighty one, and his arm shall rule for him: behold his reward is with him, and his recompense before him" (Isa. xl. 9-10, cf. lii. 7, lxi. 1). It is passages such as this that provide the background for the understanding of the words of the preaching of Jesus in Galilee: "The time is fulfilled and the Kingdom of God is at hand; repent ye, and believe in the Gospel" (Mark i. 14).

Thus the good news that Jesus proclaimed was the coming of the Reign of God. The reign had come. Both the teaching and the mighty works of the Messiah bore witness to it. The teaching unfolded the righteousness of the Kingdom, and summoned men and women to receive it. The mighty works asserted the claims of the Kingdom over the whole range of human life. The healing of the sick; the exorcism of devils; the restoration of the maimed, the deaf, the dumb, and the blind; the feeding of the hungry; the forgiveness of sinners; all these had their place among the works of the Kingdom. But though the Kingdom was indeed here in the midst of men, neither the teaching nor the mighty works could enable its coming in all its fulness. For the classic enemies—sin and death—could be dealt with only by a mightier blow, a blow which the death of the Messiah Himself alone could strike. And the righteousness of the Kingdom could not be perfected by a teaching and an example for men to follow; it involved a personal union of men with Christ Himself, a sharing in His own death and risen life. Thus He had a baptism to be baptized with, and He was straitened until it was accomplished. But when it was accomplished there was not only a Gospel in words preached by Jesus but a Gospel in deeds embodied in Jesus Himself, living, dying, conquering death. There is a hint at the identity between the Gospel of Jesus and the person of Jesus in the arresting words " for my sake and the gospel's " (Mark viii. 35, x. 29).

Thus it was that the Gospel preached by Jesus became merged into the Gospel that *is* Jesus. This is the Gospel which the Apostles preach. It is still the Gospel of God (Rom. i. 1, 2 Cor. iv. 4). It is still the Gospel of the Kingdom (Acts, *passim*). But its content is Jesus. The striking phrase " to gospel Jesus " appears (Acts v. 42, viii. 35, xi. 20). They preach His life, death, Resurrection and gift of the Spirit; for all this constitutes the drama of the mighty acts of God who came to deliver and to reign.

We are able to form some picture of the preaching of the Apostles from the speeches recorded in the Acts and from the brief summaries of the basic Christian facts which we find in the Epistles. The speeches of Peter in Jerusalem (Acts ii. 14-36; iii. 12-26, iv. 8-12) and in Caesarea (Acts x. 34-43) and of Paul at Antioch in Pisidia (Acts xiii. 16-41) disclose the common themes of the preaching. The same themes recur; and the evidence of the Epistles confirms the presence of these themes in the earliest teaching of the Church. (1) The messianic age is come, " The things which God foreshadowed by the mouth of all the prophets, He thus fulfilled." (2) This has happened through the ministry, death, and Resurrection of the Messiah. He came as David's heir. His death was not a mere tragic defeat; it was a part of God's agelong purpose for the deliverance of mankind. It was foretold in the Scriptures. By the Resurrection God vindicated the Christ. (3) Jesus, exalted at God's right hand, is Lord. He shares in the sovereignty of God. (4) His sovereignty is attested by the outpouring of Holy Spirit upon the disciples. The gift comes from the exalted Jesus Himself. (5) The end is at hand, and Jesus will return as judge of the living and the dead. This is the drama wrought by God in the events in Jerusalem whereof the Apostles are witnesses. It implies the coming of the new age, the breaking into history of the powers of the world to come. It impels the Apostles to summon men to repent and to be baptized into the name of Jesus.

Such was the Gospel. With the accounts of the preaching in Acts we can compare the tradition which Paul says that he had received (presumably from Christians in Jerusalem):

"how that Christ died for our sins according to the scriptures; and that he was buried; and that he hath been raised on the third day according to the scriptures, and that he appeared to Cephas; then to the twelve . . ." (1 Cor. xv. 3-5.)

We can compare also the allusions to the content of the Gospel in a number of passages in the Epistles (Gal. iii. 1, 1 Cor. i. 23, Rom. viii. 31-34). The Gospel was one. The same framework of events underlies the primitive preaching in Jerusalem, the preaching of Paul, the final presentation of the Gospel in the four written Gospels. There were of course differences of emphasis. Peter links the offer of forgiveness with "the name of Jesus Christ," that is with His mission and person in general; Paul links it specially with the Cross. Peter is not recorded as mentioning the burial; Paul includes it in his summary of the tradition he had received. The earliest speeches dwell upon the death and the Resurrection and say nothing of the preceding life and ministry; Peter at Caesarea includes an account of how Jesus was anointed with the Holy Spirit and went about doing good and healing all that were oppressed of the devil (Acts x. 38). But there was one Gospel. In it, amid whatever varieties, the Passion and the Resurrection had the pre-eminent place. And the whole story—ministry, Passion, Resurrection—was told not as a piece of biography but as the drama of God's mighty act as deliverer. It was not that the biographical interest in the Man Jesus came first, and a divine Gospel was subsequently deduced from it. It was that the events were from the first handed down as a divine Gospel, and only within the context of that Gospel did the biographical and human interest in Jesus survive and grow.

III

In the midst however of the Apostles' preoccupation with the Word of the Cross and with the glory of the Resurrection they did not lose sight of the earthly ministry of Jesus. Indeed their refusal to lose sight of it is impressive and significant. They knew Christ "no longer after the flesh" (cf. 2 Cor. v. 16); their immediate concern was with the contemporary Christ whom they worshipped; their message dwelt upon the absorbing and heart-rending episodes of a Crucified Messiah and a victory over death. But the words and deeds of the days of His flesh were not forgotten.

The Apostolic writers often give glimpses of the earthly ministry of Jesus. If Paul is concerned with the contemporary Christ, he recalls sayings of Jesus that have been handed down (1 Cor. vii. 10, ix. 14), and he mentions His characteristics that have been remembered—His gentleness, His forbearance, His humility and His refusal to please Himself (2 Cor. x. 1, Phil. ii. 7, Rom. xv. 2-3, cf. 1 Cor. xi. 1). If the writer of Hebrews takes for his theme the heavenly priesthood of Christ, he bids his readers contemplate the Man Jesus in His temptation, His prayers, His strong crying and tears, His godly fear, His endurance and faith. If John dwells upon the eternal Sonship, he insists also that Jesus sat by a well and was weary. The impress of the human life of Jesus rested upon the teaching of the Christians. They handed down His words and deeds, first in oral tradition and finally in written books.

But the earthly ministry was remembered, handed down and taught *never* as a self-contained biography, *always* as a part of the Gospel of God whose climax is the Passion and the Resurrection. The words and deeds of Jesus were narrated with the light of the Resurrection upon them. For the first Christians lived in a double perspective : the risen Jesus at the right hand of God and the Jesus of Galilee and Jerusalem. It is from this double perspective that all the Apostolic literature was written.

There was first the stage of *oral teaching* about Jesus. This stage has been brought into valuable prominence by the modern method of study known as Form-Criticism. The Form-critics attempt to discover, behind the Gospels, the various types of story-telling used in the early communities. Though some of their conclusions have been arbitrary and unjustifiable, they have enabled us to detect certain genuine story-forms. There was the story told for the sake of a saying of Jesus which formed its climax; there was the story told for the sake of a mighty work of Jesus which illustrated some theme of the Gospel; there was the story told in order to meet some problem or difficulty within the early Church. Thus we may picture the telling of the stories about Jesus by the preachers, teachers and catechists in the early communities. But these same communities worshipped Jesus risen from the dead. While they heard of how He healed and forgave in Galilee, they knew Him as one who healed and forgave there in their own midst. They learnt the stories not as the biographical records of a dead hero, but as illustrations of a Gospel of God, living and active and sharper than any two-edged sword, and piercing even to the dividing of soul and spirit.

After some decades there came the *Synoptic Gospels*. In them we can detect the same double perspective, the perspective of the original events that are recorded and the perspective of the worshipping Church. Do we find that the later perspective is read back into the story, and that the narratives are tinged with the devotion to the risen Jesus and with the " developed " doctrine of the Church? To some extent we find this; for while the evangelists tell of the " Rabbi " whom the disciples so addressed in Galilee they are conscious of the " Lord " of Christian doctrine and devotion after the Resurrection. Yet the impressive fact is that, taking the material in the Gospels as a whole, the " reading-back " seems so restricted and the material is often markedly " raw ": it takes us behind the Resurrection and the worshipping Church, and it shews us the original awe and bewilderment and failure of the disciples. But this material, reflecting as it does the raw reminiscence of the primitive perspective, gets its coherence and its meaning only within the Gospel of God who raised Jesus from the dead.

Thus the Gospels are works of an entirely novel and unique literary character. They are not biographies, for they pay little attention to the psychology of a hero and to many of those aspects of a life which are dear to a biographer. They are *Gospels*. They are written to tell of the events whereby the Reign of God came. The human story is told, as alone it survived to be told, in the frame of the Gospel of God. The Gospels reproduce the pattern of the preaching of the Apostles from the earliest days.

Finally there comes the *Fourth Gospel* bearing the name of John. Here the double perspective, that has been apparent at every stage of the Apostolic writings, is seen with a special and deliberate vividness.

For in this baffling and glorious book we find a blending of an emphasis upon the importance of historical fact with an emphasis upon those aspects of the truth in Jesus Christ that lie beyond the historical events. This blending of two strains puzzles the reader, and has caused the book to be regarded as a kind of problem-piece among the writings about Jesus Christ. Is the author, we ask, giving us good history, supplementing and correcting the history provided by the earlier Gospels? or is he deserting history and leading us into the realms of mystical interpretation? The problem has been baffling, for neither of these alternatives seem wholly to correspond with the author's purpose or wholly to explain all the characteristics of the book.

But when once we have perceived that the double perspective exists in all the Apostolic writings and in all the Apostolic teaching from the earliest days, then the Fourth Gospel appears in a less problematic light. For while it does indeed contain its own problems, its main problem is not a new one. It sums up the inevitable tension in Apostolic Christianity, and enables a truer understanding of that tension. John writes in order that his readers may believe that Jesus is the Christ the Son of God and believing may have life in His name. With this end in view he will not allow his readers to ignore either of the two aspects of Christianity. (1) On the one hand he makes it clear that men in every age may be in touch with Jesus Christ, risen and glorified, and may by believing on Him and feeding on Him possess eternal life. " He, the

Paraclete, shall glorify me, for He shall take of mine and shall declare it unto you." " Blessed are they that have not seen and yet have believed." The Incarnation was the prelude to the greater works that the disciples would do when Jesus had gone to the Father, and to the closer union between the disciples and Jesus made possible by His departure. Here and now men may dwell in Him, and He in them. (2) But at the same time John is at pains to shew that the contemporary Christ is known aright and that union with Him is possible, only if the Christians are in a constant relationship with the historical events of the Word-made-flesh. It is vital that the events really happened, events that men saw and heard and their hands handled. " Back to history " is an avowed motive both in the Gospel and in the First Epistle of John.

These two factors are essential to John's message. If at times he points his readers beyond history to the eternal significance of Jesus, he as often brings them to earth again with his sudden reminders of stark historical fact. But he will not let them rest in history; for the history cannot reveal God or be understood unless it points men beyond itself. Nor will he let them rest in an unhistorical mysticism, for the risen Christ, interpreted by the Paraclete, is known only by those who will believe and treasure the historical events in the flesh.

Thus John draws together the two facts which belong to Christianity from the beginning, the Jesus who lived and died in the flesh and the Jesus who is living, contemporary and life-giving. If he puzzles us by the tension between them, neither the puzzle nor the tension are of his own making. The Fourth Gospel is what it is not only because of the special tendencies and insights of the writer, but because of the nature of Christianity. From the tension between history and that which is beyond history the Christian never escapes, and within that tension the strength of Christianity lies.

The ministry, the Passion, the Resurrection, the mission of the Paraclete—John presents these in a true unity. He does so by means of the theme of *Life* which runs through his Gospel. The teaching and the works of Jesus, meeting as they do a vast variety of human needs, are united by the single purpose of bringing the gift of Life in answer to the fact of

Death, both the Death and the body and the Death of sin. Life and light are the divine answer to death and darkness. The Messiah comes that men may have life, and have it abundantly. His life-giving mission has its climax in His own death and Resurrection which enable the fullest release of life, through the Paraclete, for the disciples and for mankind. Thus John shews the unity of the mission of Christ by expounding it with the glory of the Resurrection upon it. The themes of the ministry in John are really the same in essence as those recorded in the Synoptists; but in John the light of Easter is allowed to shine backwards upon these themes, and the reader feels that this light is never absent from the story.

IV

There is yet another tension within the thought of the Apostolic Church; and this is the tension that is created by the contrast between the Crucifixion and the Resurrection. The preachers of the Gospel told their hearers of the humiliation of Jesus done to death between two criminals, and of the " exceeding greatness " of the power of God when " according to the working of the strength of his might " (Eph. i. 19) He raised Jesus from the dead. " He was crucified through weakness, yet he liveth through the power of God " (2 Cor. xiii. 4). We discover as we read the New Testament that the two events, seen first as opposites, are found increasingly to be like the two sides of a single coin. Here again it is John who finally shews us the perfect unity.

To the disciples the contrast between the Reign of God proclaimed by Jesus and the shameful death of the Messiah presented at first an unbearable paradox. But the Resurrection shewed them that the Passion was a part of the divine counsel and a prelude to glory, both for their Master and for themselves. Finally, they came to see that the Passion was not only a necessary prelude, but itself a part of the glory. This truth peeps out at many points in the Apostolic writings, until it blazes into light in the Fourth Gospel.

In the primitive preaching of the Apostles there is only a

linking of the death and the exaltation as two stages in the
divine drama. Both had their place. Jesus is both Servant and
Lord. The same linking appears in Peter's First Epistle; he
who once had stumbled at the Messiah's choice of the Cross is
now "a witness of the sufferings of Christ who am also a
partaker of the glory that shall be revealed" (1 Peter v. 1).
Paul however sees more than a linking of the two events; they
are for him blended together. The risen Christ is for ever
"the Christ who has been crucified." His theme is "Christ
Jesus that died, yea rather that was raised from the dead"
(Rom. viii. 34). Christ crucified is "the power of God and
the wisdom of God" (1 Cor. i. 24). To worship the risen
Jesus is to accept the Cross in virtue of which He triumphed :
to believe in the Crucified is to adhere to one who conquers
and reigns. Similarly the writer of Hebrews bids his readers
to "behold Jesus because of the suffering of death crowned
with glory and honour, that by the grace of God he should
taste death for every man" (Heb. ii. 9). The exact exegesis
of this verse is difficult : we cannot be quite sure whether it
speaks of Jesus as crowned with glory after His victory or as
going to His death as one who is crowned with glory already.
If Pilate's words "Behold the man" are the "Ecce Homo"
of the world which sees only the bruised figure with a crown
of thorns, these words in Hebrew are the "Ecce Homo" of
the Christian who knows where the glory really is.

This blending of Passion and Resurrection was not a piece
of picturesque dramatizing by the early Christians. It corres-
ponded to their own discovery that to share in the sufferings
of Christ was to know His triumph. They were "always
bearing about in the body the dying of Jesus that the life also
of Jesus may be manifested in our body" (2 Cor. iv. 10).

It is however in the narratives of the Passion in the Gospels
that the drawing together of the two events is most signifi-
cantly to be seen. In *Mark* the Passion is depicted as an austere
and lonely scene : the Messiah dies in utter isolation, and the
only word from the Cross is the cry "My God, my God, why
hast thou forsaken me?" Yet the scene is not one of pathos,
or tragedy or defeat. The many references to the fulfilment
of prophecy declare that here is no haphazard disaster, but
a divine act of redemption. Its power shatters the barrier

between Jew and Gentile, as is symbolized by the confession of the Roman centurion, "Truly this was the Son of God." Only the Resurrection could have so turned the darkness of Calvary into a light for the Gentiles. _Luke_ goes further in drawing Cross and Resurrection together. He shews in the Passion the serenity and the mastery of love whereby the Son of Man reaches out in sympathy and tenderness to those around Him. It is they and not He whose need and plight are pitiable. The gloom of the scene as Mark depicted it is, in Luke. lightened by the love which is already conquering. More still, Luke hints at the connection between the Cross and the glory. It is he who in the story of the Transfiguration links that scene with the Passion by telling how Moses and Elijah appeared in glory and spake of the exodus that Jesus was to fulfil in Jerusalem (Luke ix. 31). It is he who records the words spoken on the way to Emmaus: "Behoved it not the Christ to suffer these things and to enter into his glory?" (Luke xxiv. 26).

It is left to _John_ to depict the unity in full measure, and to make the explicit equation of Crucifixion and Glory. He uses the word "glory" not a few times in direct reference to the Passion; and his narrative of the Passion reflects this. In the garden the soldiers fall back, awe-struck at the Majesty of Jesus. At the trial Pilate seeks to judge Jesus, but it is Jesus who is his judge. Master of the events, Jesus carries His own Cross to Calvary, freely lays down His own life, and cries "It is finished," for the victory is His. On the Cross Jesus is King. The Crucifixion is not a defeat needing the Resurrection to reverse it, but a victory which the Resurrection quickly follows and seals. The "glory" seen in the Cross is the eternal glory of the Father and the Son; for that eternal glory is the glory of self-giving love, and Calvary is its supreme revelation.

So it is that the centre of Apostolic Christianity is _Crucifixion-Resurrection_; not Crucifixion alone nor Resurrection alone, nor even Crucifixion as the prelude and Resurrection as the finale but the blending of the two in a way that is as real to the Gospel as it is defiant to the world. The theme is implicit in the mission of Jesus as the Servant of the LORD, and it becomes increasingly explicit until John says the final word. To say that this theme is the centre of the Gospel is not to belittle the life and words of Jesus that preceded it nor the work of the Paraclete that followed it. For Life-through-Death is the principle of Jesus' whole life; it is the inward essence of the life of the Christians; and it is the unveiling of the glory of the eternal God. So utterly new and foreign to the expectations of men was this doctrine, that it seems hard to doubt that only historical events could have created it.

CHAPTER II

According to the Scriptures

THE MESSAGE of the Resurrection was the newest thing in history. Yet those who first believed it attached the utmost importance to its connection with one of the oldest things that they knew, the Scriptures of the Old Testament. This connection is still affirmed when Christians sing in the Eucharistic Creed " on the third day He rose again according to the Scriptures." Is this affirmation a tiresome survival of the Jewish atmosphere of primitive Christianity, or has it a vital place in the Gospel of the Resurrection?

Paul wrote to the Christians of Corinth to remind them of what he had originally taught them, and he hastened to say that his teaching did not originate with himself : he had " received " the form of it, handed down from an earlier tradition :

" how that Christ died for our sins according to the scriptures : and that he was buried : and that he hath been raised on the third day according to the scriptures : and that he appeared to Cephas : then to the twelve." (1 Cor. xv. 3-5.)

According to the Scriptures! The events of the Gospel were to be grasped as the fulfilment of the ancient Scriptures of the Jews. Only thus would they be truly understood. This was indeed a difficult doctrine for the people of a cosmopolitan Greek city like Corinth to swallow. They were to look to

Jewry for the understanding of the things of their salvation!
Yet, far and wide, converts to Christianity came so to do, for
the Gospel was bound up with facts and conceptions that had
their roots in the Bible of the Jews. When in the end the
Graeco-Roman world was won to Christianity it semed like
the fulfilment of an old prediction that " ten men shall take
hold, out of all the languages of the nations, shall even take
hold of the skirt of him that is a Jew, saying, We will go
with you, for we have heard the God is with you" (Zech.
viii. 23).

For the message " now hath Christ been raised from the
dead " demands that he who would understand it must think
Biblically about Christ and about Death and about Resurrection. The word Christ was more than a surname : it means the
anointed Messiah of God, and its background was the view of
history which runs through the Bible. God chose Israel to be,
in a unique way, His people : He set her free : He revealed
Himself to her by His own mighty acts, of which the climax
was the coming of the Messiah to vindicate His Kingdom and
to draw mankind within its embrace. The word Death meant
in the Bible a destiny that was specially connected with sin
and with separation from God. And the word Resurrection
when applied to the Messiah meant inevitably an act of divine
victory over both death and sin as the means of the coming
of the reign of God. Thus the Resurrection of Christ was no
isolated wonder. It was inseparable from the messianic
deliverance of mankind into the Kingdom of God.

I

The connection between Sin and Death in the Old Testament
is not confined to a theory about the fall of a historical Adam.
It lies deep and widespread in the Biblical attitude to man.
For if man is created in the image of God, in order that he may
reflect God's own attributes and live in unbroken fellowship
with God, then the true and perfect relation of God and man
will have no place for death. This is not to say that man
was once immortal, nor is it to deny that death is natural and
inevitable to man as we know him. But it is to affirm that in

the true and perfect manhood death has no place. In Jesus Christ alone both spirit and body were the perfect instrument of the Spirit of God; and some have supposed that Jesus Christ in His perfect manhood was able to pass to a heavenly glory without death, and have thought that the story of the Transfiguration suggests this. But He died because He made Himself utterly one with us and trod the road which our own maimed and mortal manhood has to tread.

Death and sin are thus linked in Biblical thought. Frequently in the Bible two aspects of death are woven together. For the word is used of the cessation of a man's existence upon earth; and it is used also of the separation from God which is, to him that believes in God, the bitterest part (cf. Psa. lxxxviii. 3-5, Isa. xxxvii. 10-18). As with death, so with life. Life means to exist upon earth as a man; and it also means to be with God (Deut. viii. 3, Isa. xxxviii. 16); for life apart from God barely deserves the name of life at all. This interviewing of the religious and the physical aspects of death and life is one of the distinctive glories of the Biblical view of man. It provides the background for a corresponding belief about the redemption wrought by Jesus Christ; for in this redemption the conquest of death is linked with the conquest of sin, and the bestowal of everlasting life is linked with the bestowal of fellowship with God. In the reign of God there will be no more death, only because the spirits and bodies of men shall be freed from sin and made alive unto God.

It was in these terms that the Gospel concerning Jesus Christ was proclaimed and understood. The death of Christ was seen in relation to the Biblical meaning of death. It was the deepest point of His loving identification of Himself with mankind. He put Himself beside them, He went the whole way with them, He shared in the darkness of their self-sought separation from God. He plunged beneath the waters of their calamity. But He was raised from death so as to bring to the Father a life that is for ever alive unto God: " the life that he liveth, he liveth unto God." The self-centredness of human life and death finds its answer in Jesus Christ who lives because, and only because, He lives unto God. The victory over death is inseparable from the victory over sin; and the risen Christ is a revelation of manhood finding its perfect end in the life unto God, with spirit and body glorified in perfect obedience to the Spirit of God.

This victory was won in order that the human race might share in it. "Likewise reckon ye yourselves to be dead indeed unto sin but alive unto God through Jesus Christ our Lord." It was not that Christ's Resurrection exemplified an immortality that belongs to all men as they are. It was that He enabled men to be released from sin and death through union with Him, and to become sharers in *His* Resurrection. Their entry into His Resurrection is both here and hereafter. The first Christians knew that they had already become "raised together with Christ" (Col. iii. 1). But they believed also that a fuller entry awaited them after their death, for there would be a final resurrection unto their final destiny. They still must die, for death remains as long as the world shall last. But it remains only as an enemy defeated and spoiled of his power. It is no longer the last word. It has become a road along which those who are Christ's may pass to a fuller sharing in His life.

Thus the Resurrection of Christ meant far more than the addition of a new doctrine concerning the future state to the doctrines which had been held before. It concerned the whole relation of mankind to God and of God to mankind. It was an act that summed up God's purpose in history, conquered sin and death, wrought a new principle of life for this world no less than for the next, and vindicated the righteousness of the God of the Bible. Thus when many of the people of Corinth came to believe in the Resurrection of Christ, they were embracing not just a new idea about immortality but a belief in the God of Israel and the salvation which He had wrought. His Resurrection is the means of mankind's release from *its own* sin and death into *His own* life-unto-God both in this age and in the age to come.

II

The words "according to the Scriptures" had these big implications. But, immediately, they meant the fulfilment of certain passages in the Old Testament. The Resurrection sent the Apostles back to their Bible. There they could see the meaning of the new and marvellous happening. There they could find its relation to the age-long purposes of God.

The Jews had never expected that the Messiah would suffer and die, and thus they had never expected that He would rise again. They never included within their Messianic expectations the description of the sufferings of the Servant of the LORD in Isaiah liii. To them, there were no Scriptures that foretold either the Messiah's death or the Messiah's Resurrection. Nor had the idea of His Resurrection entered seriously into the expectation of the disciples of Jesus (cf. Mark ix. 10). It seems that the predictions of Jesus gave them no clear conviction, and right up to Easter morning they did not think that the Scriptures in any way foretold the Resurrection. Yet, when once the event had happened, they leaped to the belief that in the raising of Jesus from death the Scriptures had been fulfilled, and they proclaimed the belief to their fellow-Jews.

Of what Scriptures were the Apostles thinking? They had in mind proof-texts which they discovered, some of which may seem to us to be used in ways remote from their original meaning. But that was not all. Beneath the use of proof-texts was the conviction that the whole story of God's words and actions in Israel had found its climax and its key in the death and Resurrection of Christ. In Scott Holland's words, "The entire body of ancient Scripture opened its heart to the astonished and rejoicing Apostles" (op. cit., p. 28).

(1) The proof-texts appear often in the preaching of the Apostles. For the death of Christ, the fifty-third chapter of Isaiah, with its description of the Servant of the LORD who suffered and bare the sin of many, came quickly into use. For the Resurrection, a variety of passages were used. There was a passage from the sixteenth Psalm, quoted by Peter at Pentecost and by Paul in Antioch in Pisidia (Acts ii. 25-28, xiii. 35):

" I beheld the LORD always before my face;
　For he is on my right hand, that I should not be moved;
　Therefore my heart was glad, and my tongue rejoiced :
　Moreover my flesh also shall rejoice in hope;
　Because thou wilt not leave my soul in Hades,
　neither wilt thou give thy Holy One to see corruption :
　Thou madest known unto me the ways of life :
　Thou shalt make me full of gladness with thy countenance."
(Psa. xvi. 8-11.)

There was also a passage from the one hundred and eighteenth Psalm :

　　" The stone which the builders rejected
　　　is become the head of the corner.
　　This is the LORD'S doing :
　　　it is marvellous in our eyes.
　　This is the day which the LORD hath made :
　　　we will rejoice and be glad in it."
(Psa. cxviii. 22-24 quoted Acts iv. 11, 1 Peter ii. 7.)

Yet another Psalm was quoted in reference to the vindication of Jesus by the Resurrection as Son of God :

" thou art my Son : this day I have begotten thee." (Psa. ii. 7.)

As to the exaltation of Jesus to heaven, which followed the Resurrection and is sometimes hardly separated from it in thought, the Apostolic writers make frequent use of Psalm cx :

" The LORD said unto my Lord,
　Sit thou on my right hand,
　until I make thine enemies thy footstool." (Psa. cx. 1.)

This Psalm was quoted by Jesus (Mark xii. 36). It was used by Peter (Acts ii. 34); and the imagery of " the right hand of God " recurs again and again in the Apostolic writings. In all these ways the Scriptures, in the belief of the Apostles, " testified beforehand the sufferings of Christ, and the glories that should follow them " (1 Peter i. 11).

Did the Apostles also use proof-texts for the occurrence of the Resurrection *on the third day*? Here the evidence available is very slight. The New Testament contains no actual citation of any proof-text upon this point. The possible references in the Old Testament to a Resurrection on the third day are few and elusive (cf. Jonah i. 17, Hosea vi. 2, 2 Kings xx. 5); and it is therefore unlikely that the Old Testament passages can have created the belief that the Resurrection occurred on the third day. It is far more probably that the event, attested by good evidence, created any use of proof-texts that was made. As to such use of texts, it is possible—some would say it is probable—that the Apostles made use of Hosea's words :

> "Come, and let us return unto the Lord;
> For he hath torn, and he will heal us :
> He hath smitten, and he will bind us up.
> After two days will he revive us;
> On the third day he will raise us up,
> And we shall live before him." (Hosea vi. 1-2.)

There is also recorded in Matthew a saying of Jesus.

> "as Jonah was three days and three nights in the belly of the whale : so shall the Son of man be three days and three nights in the heart of the earth." (Matt. xii. 40.)

These words may be an elaboration of a simpler saying about the sign of Jonah that occurs in the primitive source (cf. Luke xi. 29-32). They suggest in God's deliverance of Jonah from his plight a comparison with God's raising of Christ from death. There is no decisive reason why Jesus should not have spoken them.

(2) It was however not only in terms of proof-texts that the Apostles were thinking. There was a larger fact that lay beneath the use of these texts. The particular passages had their significance because the Scriptures *as a whole* had found fulfilment. What God did of old time, in the call and redemption of Israel, in the catastrophes and deliverances of her history, has now found its climax in the deliverance of Christ from death.

Throughout the Old Testament there had been the strain of a tension which, it seemed, could never be resolved. On the one hand there was the faith of Israel in God's sovereignty and righteousness and faithfulness to His people. On the other hand there were the sufferings of the righteous and the cries of the afflicted. The tension ran through the history of Israel, and it sometimes strained the faith of Israel nearly to the point of breaking. But, now that the Christ has Himself suffered and been raised from death, the tension within the Scriptures is resolved and the unity of the Scriptures has been disclosed. For it is perceived that the sufferings of the Servant of the LORD do not contradict the sovereign power of God; rather are those sufferings the means whereby God has wrought mightily in His purpose to deliver mankind.

Thus the Scriptures, being vindicated by Jesus Christ, seem in divers ways to speak about Him. Passages about the sufferings of the righteous seem to describe His Passion (cf. Psa. xxii.). Passages about God's mighty deliverances seem to bear witness to His Resurrection. The Old Testament is found both to foretell Christ and to preach Him.

If the reader will turn to the speech of S. Paul at Antioch in Pisidia (Acts xiii. 16-41) he will see a clear illustration of the two aspects of fulfilment. There is in this speech the characteristic use of proof-texts. S. Paul cites Psa. ii., Psa. xvi., Isa. lv. 3 and Hab. i. 5 in his preaching of the Resurrection. But there is also in this speech that which underlies the use of proof texts, namely the conviction of the unity of God's acts in Israel and his acts in Christ.

" Men of Israel, and ye that fear God, hearken. The God of this people Israel *chose* our fathers, and *exalted* the people when they sojourned in the land of Egypt, and with a high arm he *led them forth* out of it. . . . He *gave* them their land . . . he *gave* them judges . . . he *gave* unto them Saul the Son of Kish . . . he *raised up* David to be their king . . . he *brought* unto Israel a Saviour Jesus . . . God *raised him from the dead*. . . . And we bring unto you good tidings of the promise made unto the fathers, how that God hath fulfilled the same unto our children, in that he raised up Jesus. . . . Beware therefore, lest that come upon you, which is spoken in the prophets:

"Behold, ye despisers and wonder and perish:
For I work a work in your days,
A work which ye shall in no wise believe, if one declare it unto you."

For the God of Irsael is a God who "raises up." In divers ways the word "raise up" is used of His acts in the Old Testament. He raised up prophets, judges, the poor, the nation, the fallen tabernacle of David (Amos ix. 11), a righteous branch (Jer. xxiii. 5), a shepherd in the land (Zech. xi. 16). Israel's history is misunderstood if it is treated primarily as a story of human genius gradually advancing in its ideas about God. It is God who acts, speaking, calling, delivering. The history of Israel is a series of crises wherein in hours of catastrophe God stretches out His arm in judgment and mercy. Finally a day comes when Jesus Christ, identifying Himself with Israel, bears the destiny of Israel with Him to the Cross and the grave; and God raises Him, and with Him Israel, from out of death.

The central theme of the Apostles was not belief in the Resurrection, so much as belief in the God who raised up Jesus. As we have seen, to be a Christian was "to believe on him who raised up Jesus our Lord from the dead" (Rom. iv. 24, cf. 1 Peter i. 21) and New Testament theism is essentially Resurrection-theism. It is sometimes said that the one really important fact is that the life of Jesus continues, and therefore the act whereby this was effected cannot greatly matter. It is indeed impossible to exaggerate the importance of the fact that the life of Jesus continues, and the Apostles dwelt upon this fact constantly. But it was not all that mattered. God had raised Him up, and the Apostles dwelt upon this act of raising; ὁ Θεὸς ἤγειρεν, Χριστὸς ἠγέρθη, those are the characteristic words used.[1] For the act of raising reveals the

[1] Throughout the New Testament the Resurrection is most often described not as Jesus raising Himself but as Jesus being raised or as God raising Him. A notable exception is John x. 17, "I lay down my life that I may take it again."

God of Israel, the God who raises from death, the living God
as yet unknown to Athens and Corinth. The Christians came
to know

> " the exceeding greatness of his power to usward who
> believe, according to that working of the strength of his
> might which he wrought in Christ, when he raised him
> from the dead." (Eph. i. 19-20.)

III

It is not therefore surprising that the Apostles described the
Resurrection by likening it to two of the greatest acts of the
power of God of which they could read in the Old Testament.
God created the world : God led Israel out of Egypt in the
Exodus. The Apostles believed that they were witnesses of a
new Exodus of Israel, and a new act of creation as moment-
ous as when God said, Let there be light : and there was
light.

The New Exodus

In Luke's account of the Transfiguration we read that " there
talked with him two men which were Moses and Elijah; who
appeared in glory and *spake about his exodus* which he was
about to fulfil in Jerusalem " (ix. 30-31). The Greek word
used is " exodus." The word can mean a man's departure in
death, and in the Authorized Version and Revised Version it
is here translated " decease." But its normal meaning is
simply " going-forth," or " exodus," and such may be the
suggestion here. It was of an Exodus of Israel that Moses and
Elijah spoke. The Passion, foretold by Jesus six days before,
would be the prelude to a new Exodus of the people of God
from bondage to freedom.

Such was the belief of the Apostles. Israel in rejecting the
Messiah brought doom upon herself. But the Messiah was
raised from death to be the head of a new Israel, a spiritual

race and nation. As the old Israel looked back to the Exodus from Egypt and kept the Passover to commemorate God's deliverance, so the new Israel looks back to the Exodus from sin and death in the Passion and Resurrection and commemorates God's deliverance in the sacrament of the Body and Blood of Christ.

Thus Peter in his First Epistle reminds his readers that they are participants in a new Exodus. He begins with an outburst of praise for the Resurrection, whereby the Christians were begotten again unto a living hope unto an inheritance in heaven. They have been set free by the blood of Christ, as their fathers believed themselves to have been set free by the lamb of the Passover (i. 18-19). They are, like Israel of old, " an elect race, a royal priesthood, a holy nation, a people for God's own possession " (ii. 9). Paul gives essentially the same picture. The passing through the sea, the eating of the manna from heaven, the drinking of the water from the rock, all have their greater counterpart in the new Exodus of the Christians (cf. 1 Cor. x. 1-4). It is the same God who has wrought deliverance; and from Apostolic times the Church of Christ has found in the Psalms about the Exodus a fitting language for the praises of the God of Israel who is still their God and has led them forth by Jesus Christ, the shepherd raised from death (cf. Heb. xiii. 20).

> " Thy way was in the sea,
>   And thy paths in the great waters
>   And thy footsteps were not known,
>   Thou leadest thy people like a flock
>   By the hand of Moses and Aaron." (Psa. lxxvii. 19-20.)

The New Creation

It was more than a new Exodus which the Apostles found in the Resurrection. It was the begetting of a new race, and the creation of a new world. These things were wrought by the Holy Spirit bestowed by the risen Jesus : they were the immediate impact of the Resurrection.

Here again the Epistle of Peter tells of the new belief. The Resurrection was the source of a new-begetting.

"Blessed be the God and Father of our Lord Jesus Christ who according to his great mercy begat us again unto a living hope by the resurrection of Jesus Christ from the dead." (1 Peter i. 3.)

"S. Peter's language," wrote Dr. Hort in his commentary, "includes the conception of entrance into a new order of existence but combines with it that of a divine parentage: men enter the new life as children of its author." "The hope is living," writes Fr. Thornton, "because it springs up in the new life to which we have been begotten again; and this took place through the resurrection. Our Lord's resurrection is doubtless 'instrumental in our rebirth, because it guarantees both his Messiahship and our immortality.' But this is not simply a forceful way of saying that 'hope was reborn in us.' For the resurrection of Christ was something more than a guarantee of Christian truths. The resurrection was the historical channel through which God acted when he begat us again" (*The Common Life in the Body of Christ,* p. 197).

The new birth or begetting is realised in the rite of Christian baptism. It is wrought by the Holy Spirit; it is received by the repentance and faith of the convert: but the impact of the Resurrection alone makes it possible. For the Resurrection both asserts the lordship of Jesus beneath which the convert passes into his new life; and it enables the convert to share in the risen life of Jesus. This relation includes the gift of sonship, for it is the emphatic teaching of the New Testament that men *become* sons of God through the action of the Holy Spirit who reproduces Christ's sonship in them (Rom. viii. 14-15, John i. 12). Christ is thus "the firstborn among many brethren" (Rom. viii. 29); but He is so only because He is "the firstborn from the dead" (Col. i. 18). The great doctrine that Christ is the Second Adam, the author of a new humanity that is being moulded into His own true image, has its basis in the Resurrection. "The first man Adam became a living soul. The last Adam became a life-giving spirit" (1 Cor. xv. 45). The original man possessed the life that God gave to him, but the New Man Christ bestows life upon mankind. A new birth, a new sonship, a new race have their origin in the Resurrection of Christ.

This tremendous language, used by the Apostolic writers, shews that they believe the Resurrection to be not merely a great event upon the plane of history, but an act that breaks into history with the powers of another world. It is akin to the creation in the beginning; and the Gospel is the good news that God is creating a new world.

> " For we preach not ourselves, but Christ Jesus as Lord and ourselves as your servants for Jesus' sake. Seeing it is God, that said, Light shall shine out of darkness, who shined in our hearts, to give the light of the knowledge of the glory of God in the face of Jesus Christ." (2 Cor. iv. 5-6.)

These words recall the dazzling light that confronted Paul at his conversion. He comes to know that this light betokens a new creation. God spake, and it was done. He spake in the mission, death and Resurrection of Jesus,

> " Wherefore if any man is in Christ there is a new creation; the old things are passed away, behold they are become new." (2 Cor. v. 17.)

A new world has dawned, and the Christians belong to it already.

It is not only the spiritual aspect of man that is affected by the Resurrection. In face of the contemporary Hellenistic teaching that the body is irrelevant and is to be left behind in the interests of a purely spiritual salvation, the first Christians insisted that the body, created by God, is also redeemed by God. The body is for the Lord.

> " if the Spirit of him that raised up Jesus from the dead dwelleth in you, he that raised up Christ Jesus from the dead shall quicken also your mortal bodies through his Spirit that dwelleth in you." (Rom. viii. 11.)

Both here and hereafter the bodies of the Christians share in the effects of Christ's victory over death.[1] Nor is it man alone that is embraced by the Resurrection; for the deliverance of mankind will be the prelude to the freeing of nature from its present frustration, and

> "the creation itself also shall be delivered from the bondage of corruption into the liberty of the glory of the children of God." (Rom. viii. 21.)

The liturgies of Eastern Christendom have echoed the Apostolic belief that all the world is destined to share in the new creation wrought by the Resurrection

> "For meet it is that the heavens should rejoice : and that the earth should be glad, and that the whole world, both visible and invisible, should keep the Feast. For Christ is risen, the everlasting joy.
>
> "Now all things are filled with light, heaven and earth and all the places under the earth. All creation doth celebrate the Resurrection of Christ.
>
> "Rejoice, O creation, and bloom like a lily! For Christ as God has risen from the dead! O death, where is thy sting? O grave, where is thy victory?
>
> "As God thou didst arise from the grave in glory, and with thee didst raise the world."

It was in no spirit of dream or of phantasy that the Apostles dared to say that a new creation was being wrought. They were not weaving an academic doctrine or spinning an apocalyptic theory. They were missionaries, immersed in the practical tasks of their calling and grimly realistic about the state of the hostile world. But they knew that in the Resurrection of Christ another world had come, and that they were already its citizens; and they summoned men to enter it with them and to claim it as their own. The old world continued with its contradictions and its sufferings, but by the Cross and the Resurrection these very contradictions and

---

[1] The implications of the "bodily resurrection" of the Christians are discussed in chapter viii of this book.

sufferings could be transformed into things fruitful and creative wherein, by faith in the Crucified, the power of God might be found. There was no escaping from the facts of this world. Rather did their membership within the world-to-come enable them to see the facts of this world with the light of the Cross and the Resurrection upon them, and to know that their own tasks were but the working out of a victory that Christ had already won.

All this had been wrought by the God of their fathers and their Scriptures. It was the Lord's doing, and it was marvellous in their eyes.

CHAPTER III

History and Belief

I

THE THEOLOGY of the Apostles sprang, as we have seen, not from their own theorizing, but from certain historical events which led them to beliefs far removed from their own preconceived notions. The most significant of the events was the Resurrection. What sort of event was this? What in fact happened? Before we turn, as turn we must, to the direct historical evidence, we may ask: What sort of event is postulated by the message which we have seen to pervade the teaching and writing of the Apostles?

Clearly the Apostles' message rested upon an event of *Resurrection* as distinct from an event of *survival*. The distinction is big and important, between a Resurrection and the survival of an immortal soul. In the Platonist doctrine of immortality the body dies, but the soul continues its life. Thus, really and essentially, there is no death for that aspect of man that is deemed to be of eternal importance; the truth is that " in the sight of the unwise they *seem* to have died." Very different is a belief that the continuing life of the soul by itself is a maimed and incomplete life, that death is real with no semblance attaching to it, that Resurrection is the raising from out of death of a life that will be as rich and richer in the unity of soul and body than the life that existed previous to death.

Now the central theme of the Apostolic teaching is bound up with the belief not that Jesus spiritually survived, but that Jesus was raised. (1) He truly died. He underwent, so both the Gospels and the Epistles tell us, the whole fact of death in all its bitterness. His soul was exceeding sorrowful even unto death. He tasted of death for sinners, making Himself one with them. He took upon Himself the reality of death in its connection with sin. The death was real and complete. If it could be said of Jesus that " in the sight of the unwise He seemed to have died " and that His essential and complete life survived from the hour of the Crucifixion, then the central theme of the Apostolic Gospel would be rendered void and false. (2) Further, it is not only the continuing life of the risen Jesus that matters supremely in New Testament Christianity. For besides the emphasis upon " Jesus Christ the same, yesterday, to-day, and for ever " there is in the Apostolic teaching an equal emphasis upon the *act* of God in raising Him. It is the *act* that reveals the power of the living God; and the Christian life is lived in relation to this initial *act* no less than in relation to the contemporary presence of Jesus. (3) Further, the event upon which the Gospel rests is unique, redemptive, creative. It is not that Jesus Christ by surviving death demonstrates that all good men survive it too. The Resurrection is far more than an illustration or an example of human immortality. It is a victory uniquely won, and won in order that mankind may be enabled to share in *Christ's* Resurrection. It does for us what we cannot do for ourselves.

The Gospel therefore postulates as its basis not an illustration of survival but a miracle of Resurrection. Its character as a miracle does not depend upon any portentous happenings that may have accompanied it nor upon its being a " bodily " as distinct from a " spiritual " act. The Resurrection is a miracle because it is a unique redemptive and creative intervention of God; it interrupts the hitherto normal workings of historical cause and effect and the hitherto normal workings of the order of human sinfulness, and ushers in a new stage in the cosmic process. "It is evident," wrote Westcott "that if the claim to be a miraculous religion is essentially incredible, Apostolic Christianity is simply false."

A miracle may be called an event wrought by God which does not fit into the hitherto observable laws of nature. It resembles in one way the actions of the free wills of men which disturb the dispositions of nature; and it resembles in another way the operations of the grace of God in human lives. It is credible to those who, recognizing the potentialities of free will in man to distort the divine design, do not deny to the living God His own freedom in His work as redeemer. If the Resurrection breaks what appears to be law, it does so in order to vindicate another and a higher aspect of law. As a miracle, it is the disclosure of an order of being new, unknown, transcendental. It is, in the literal sense of the word, a " revelation " : it unveils a new level of glorified human life.

Yet though it is a miracle in relation to the observable laws of the world that we know, the Resurrection is, in relation to the new order that it discloses, natural, inevitable, lawful. It shews us perfect human nature glorified through a perfect response to the Spirit of God. It shews us the goal for which human nature was created, and to which it will be raised when the law of the Spirit of life in Christ Jesus sets men free from the law of sin and death (cf. Rom. viii. 2). It shews us both the crown of the purpose of God in the Scriptures, and the crown of His purpose in the created world, wherein new levels of life succeed to old levels and the series of successions arouses what Butler called " the implicit hope of something further."

The miracle of the Resurrection could thus be made known only to those who responded to the new level of spiritual existence which it disclosed. It was not a portent which could be shewn to all and sundry to scare them into belief. Westcott's classic words are worth quoting :

" If then the life of the risen Lord had been simply a renovation or a continuance of the former life, subject to the same conditions and necessarily destined to the same inevitable close, then the experience of unbelievers would have been sufficient to test, the witness of unbelievers would have been adequate to establish the reality of the Resurrection. But if it was a foreshadowing of new powers of human action, of a new mode of human being, then without a corresponding power of spiritual discernment there could be no testimony to its truth. The world could not see Christ, and Christ could not—there is a divine impossibility—shew Himself to the world. To have proved by incontestable evidence that Christ rose again as Lazarus rose again would have been not to confirm our faith, but to destroy it irretrievably." (*Revelation of the Risen Lord,* pp. 11-12.)

There was in the Resurrection a gentleness and a restraint akin to that which was seen in the ministry and in the Passion.

This is not to say that the appeal to historical evidence is unimportant. On the contrary, the evidence is of great importance. It may be shewn that certain historical facts are unaccountable apart from the Resurrection, and that different lines of historical testimony so converge as to point to the Resurrection with overwhelming probability. But decisive proof can never be provided. Belief in the Resurrection, involving as it does the most strict historical considerations, involves also belief in Jesus Christ.

The narratives in the Gospels suggest that a number of factors played their part in leading the Apostles to their belief. It was not the news of the empty tomb alone that convinced them: of itself this news seemed to them to be idle talk. There was need besides the empty tomb for the appearances of Jesus; and here far more was involved than proof by means of visible phenomena. There was the gradual impact of the risen Jesus upon their minds and consciences; and there was the unfolding of the Scriptures so that what they heard and saw became integrated with their faith in God and His righteous purpose for mankind. The tomb, the appearances, the converse of Jesus, the Scriptures—all these had their place in leading the Apostles through fear to wonder, through wonder to faith, and through faith to worship. For their belief included not only a conviction that a certain event had happened, but faith in the God who wrought it and in the Crucified Jesus whom it vindicated.

II

The historical evidence now demands examination. If apologists have sometimes made the mistake of seeking to " prove " the Resurrection, and if historical critics have sometimes made the mistake of investigating the history without due appreciation of the theology with which it was linked from the very first, it would be a no less grievous mistake to rest in theological affirmations and to belittle the scope of scientific historical inquiry. It is by their readiness to welcome such inquiry and to participate in it that the teachers of Christianity make good their claim that the Gospel rests upon fact.

In this chapter therefore the main elements in the historical evidence for the Resurrection will be described : and in the chapters that follow there will be some account of the trend of modern investigation and some fresh examination of the chief problems presented by the narratives in the Gospels.

What is the evidence? It might be claimed that the Apostolic Gospel, which we have already been studying in this book, is in itself evidence, for it bears no marks of having originated in theory or speculation and it bears many marks of having originated in events that created it and gave it its distinctive character. What however is the more direct evidence which the historian must investigate?

(1) It is important first to notice that the Resurrection was not expected. The available evidence suggests that neither the Scriptures nor the words of Jesus had led the disciples to a conviction that He would rise again. If the predictions by Jesus of His Passion went home to the disciples, the predictions of the Resurrection (if indeed He made such predictions explicitly) caused no clear expectation.

There are first the three " formal " predictions of the Resurrection recorded by Mark. Thrice, after foretelling the Passion, Jesus is said to have added the words " and after three days rise again" (Mark viii. 31, iv. 31, x. 34). Matthew and Luke, in editing the passages, alter the words "after three days" to "on the third day."[1] The predictions are full of detail, mentioning the delivery of Jesus by the Jews to the Gentiles, the mocking, the scourging, the Crucifixion, the Resurrection. It is possible, as many scholars are inclined to think, that the words have been elaborated and formalized in the light of knowledge after the event.

Yet it is likely that predictions of a rising again were made by Jesus. Mark ix. 10 depicts the disciples "questioning among themselves what the rising again from the dead should mean"; and besides the three "formal" predictions there are other more allusives ones. (1) There is the injunction not to make known the Transfiguration "save when the Son of Man should have risen again from the dead" (Mark ix. 9). (2) There is the saying on the night before the Passion "howbeit, after I am raised up, I will go before you into Galilee" (Mark xiv. 28). (3) There is a puzzling saying, in answer to a warning that Herod seeks to kill Him, "Behold, I cast out devils and perform cures to-day and to-morrow, and the third day I am perfected" (Luke xiii. 32), a saying which may originally have had no reference to the rising-again on the third day. (4) There is the saying, peculiar to Matthew, where the coming burial of Jesus in the earth is likened to the sojourn of Jonah for three days and nights in the belly of a whale (Matt. xii. 40, contrast Luke xi. 29-30). If genuine, this saying might have conveyed to the disciples no more than that there would be for Jesus a humiliation and a deliverance akin to that of Jonah of old. (5) There was also the saying recorded in the Fourth Gospel, "Destroy this temple, and in three days I will raise it up" (John ii. 18-19), a saying that has a counterpart in the Synoptists who record that Jesus at His trial was accused of threatening to destroy the temple and to build another in three days (Mark xiv. 58). As we shall see, the saying anticipates the destruction of the old order

---

[1] There is evidence that the phrase "the third day" sometimes bore the meaning of "a very short time," i.e. before a visitor had become a resident or before a dead body had begun to suffer decay. Thus it is possible that Jesus so used the phrase as to convey to the disciples that death and defeat would after a very short space be followed by victory. Cf. John xvi. 17, "a little while, and ye shall see me."

symbolized by the temple and its replacement by the risen Christ with His Body and Temple, the new Israel. Such are the predictions which the Gospels record.

The predictions are mysterious, elusive: the more so because Jesus made predictions in other kinds of imagery too. He spoke of the coming of the Son of Man in glory (Mark xiv. 62), of the coming of the Kingdom of God in power (Mark ix. 1), of the banquet in the Kingdom of God with the disciples (Mark xiv. 25), of "that day" (Luke x. 12), of the "day of the Son of Man (Matt. xxiv. 27-39, Luke xvii. 26-27), as well as of a rising "on the third day." Perhaps the varied imagery depicted one and the same event, a coming of the Reign of God into history in a manner that defied exact description. A divine victory was coming, beyond the Passion. But meanwhile the disciples were, it seems, left bewildered as to what to expect. The predictions of the Passion filled their minds with dark forebodings; and beyond this point their minds could hardly move.

The disciples were not anticipating the Resurrection. It is possible to dismiss at the outset any view that their belief in it sprang from a projection of their own expectations.

(2) Next, there is the evidence provided by the existence of the Church in spite of the catastrophe of Good Friday. What happened, so as to change the disciples from survivors of a cause that was broken and crushed into men who could bid the nation to repent and be baptized into the name of Christ, and could proclaim even the Crucifixion itself to be a Gospel?

This is a question that the historian cannot avoid. If he advances the hypothesis that the disciples were led to imagine a great event by the projection of their own hopes and preconceptions, he will be met by the evidence that the belief in the Resurrection stretched the disciples far beyond their own presuppositions and turned these presuppositions upside down. If he advances the hypothesis that the personality of Jesus had so gripped them and His teaching had so influenced them that they were unable to think of Him as dead and gone and were convinced that He lived on, he will be met by the evidence that the centre of their preaching was not the personality and teaching of Jesus but the Cross and the Resurrection. It must not be forgotten that the teaching and ministry of Jesus did not provide the disciples with a Gospel, and led them from puzzle to paradox until the Resurrection gave them a key. The whole claim of Jesus to proclaim and to embody the Reign of God breaks down in deceit or in failure if Calvary is the end. Without the Resurrection the historian has the problem of Jesus, no less than the problem of the Church, to explain.

(3) There is the evidence that the disciples became subject to the impact of Jesus Christ moulding their minds and hearts. This is evidence from religious experience, and it is beset by the difficulties and limitations which belong to such evidence. But evidence it is. In the case of Saul of Tarsus the impact began while he was persecuting the disciples of the crucified Jesus. He records the reversal that he underwent : the revolution of his entire relation to God, to Christ, to the world, and to himself. He exemplified this revolution in every part of a life of action, thought and suffering; and he ascribed it to an unwanted and unexpected act of Christ. "For neither did I receive it from man, neither was I taught it, but it came to me through revelation of Jesus Christ" (Gal. i. 12); "I was apprehended by Christ Jesus" (Phil. iii. 12). The testimony cannot easily be dismissed, for it is corroborated by the testimony of other Apostles, and it is related not to a narrow field of religion or emotion but to the whole of a life wherein thinking, feeling and action were made creative under the new and unexpected impulse.

(4) There is the evidence that Jesus appeared to the disciples. We find this evidence in Paul's statements about himself, in the tradition that Paul received concerning other Apostles, and in the narratives in the Gospels.

Paul distinguishes the appearances of the risen Jesus to him from visions of a mystical sort which he had at other times. He sometimes experienced "visions and revelations of the Lord" and in one of these he was caught up into the third heaven (2 Cor. xii. 2). He was careful to attach small importance to these experiences and to be reticent about them. But he speaks in a totally different manner about the claim that, at the beginning of his discipleship, he saw Jesus. It was an appearance of Jesus akin to the appearances to the other Apostles (1 Cor. xv. 8). "Am I not an apostle? Have

I not seen Jesus Christ?" (1 Cor. ix. 1). He could not be
reticent about that appearance of Jesus which was the basis
of his mission and his authority.

The accounts of Paul's conversion in the Acts (chs. ix.,
xxii., xxvi.) differ from one another in some details, but they
are congruous with Paul's own evidence in his Epistles and
they " really present a perfectly harmonious picture, that Saul
beheld an external vision of Christ in His risen glory; that
it came to him suddenly and without; that it was so far from
his thoughts and anticipations that he utterly failed to recognize who it was that appeared before him; that it was only in
answer to his bewildered exclamation ' who art thou, Lord?'
that he was told ' I am Jesus of Nazareth whom thou persecutest '; that he trembled and was astonished, and in utter help-
lessness appealed for further knowledge, ' Lord, what wilt
thou have me to do?' " (Sparrow-Simpson: *Our Lord's
Resurrection,* pp. 117-118).

But it is not only to the appearance of Jesus to himself
that Paul refers. He records, and amplifies, the primitive
tradition of the appearances to the eleven and to others. He
gives the " list " in 1 Corinthians xv.

" he appeared to Cephas: then to the twelve: then he
appeared unto five hundred brethren at once, of whom the
greater part remain until now, but some are fallen asleep:
then he appeared to James: then to all the apostles: and
last of all, as unto one born out of due time, he appeared
to me also." (1 Cor. xv. 5-8.)

It is not clear at what point in this list Paul is passing from
the primitive tradition to supplementary information of his
own. But plainly the appearances to Cephas and to the twelve
belong to the primitive tradition. Paul would have learnt this
tradition when he made his first visit to Jerusalem after his
conversion and saw Peter, possibly not more than nine years
after the Crucifixion. Here indeed is early evidence. It is not
surprising that the tradition, in the brief form here used,
makes no mention of the appearances to the women, for it
was the testimony of the Apostles that would be held to have
a special authority. To the Corinthians, mention of the evi-

dence of women quite unknown to them would carry little
weight.

The evidence here cited by Paul appears some decades
later in ampler form in the narratives in the Gospels. The
appearance to Cephas is alluded to in Luke; the appearance
to the Apostles is described by Luke and John; an appearance
to a larger number of disciples in Galilee is described by
Matthew; there is no mention of an appearance to James.

(5) There is, lastly, the evidence that the women found
the tomb empty upon the third day after the Crucifixion and
reported the news to the Apostles. This evidence is set forth
in the Gospels. Mark describes the visit of the women; John
follows a separate tradition of a visit by Mary Magdalene
alone. According to John—and some MSS. of Luke—Apostles
came to the tomb to verify the news for themselves.

There is no reference to this evidence in documents earlier
than the Gospels; and the question arises, Did the empty
tomb have a place in the primitive tradition? It seems that
although the primitive tradition as we know it does not mention the *evidence* about the empty tomb, it none the less
implied the belief in it. The words of the tradition, as Paul
reproduces it, seem incomprehensible unless they mean that
the body of Jesus was raised up.

" how that Christ died . . . and that he was buried . . . and
that he hath been raised again on the third day."

Died—buried—raised : the words are used very strangely
unless they mean that what was buried was raised up. What
otherwise is the point of the reference to the burial? In
default of the very strongest evidence that Paul meant something different and was using words in a most unnatural way,
the sentence must refer to a raising up of the body. The most
radical of critics, Schmiedel, and the most scientific of critics,
Lake, agreed that the *belief* in the empty tomb is implied in
these words.

It is however sometimes said that Paul cannot have known
of the evidence about the discovery of the empty tomb, or
else he would have alluded to this evidence in Corinthians
xv. This suggestion was long ago answered by Lake:

" Was there any reason why S. Paul should have supplied these details had he known them? Surely not. He was not trying to convince the Corinthians that the Lord was risen : he was reminding them that he had already convinced them " (*The Historical Evidence for the Resurrection of Jesus Christ*, p. 194). It is therefore impossible to draw any conclusion that Paul must or must not have known about the women's story. What is clear is that the tradition as he received it meant the death and the burial and the raising up of Jesus from the tomb. But the evidence for the empty tomb is not here cited ; and it is only in the Gospels that we find it set forth.

Such are the main factors in the evidence for the Resurrection. The event itself no man saw, and no evangelist has dared to describe, though the writer of the Apocryphal " Gospel of Peter " so dared. But the evidence that points to the event is the existence of the Church, the experience of the earliest Christians, the records of the appearances of Jesus, and the records of the empty tomb. Though the evidence about the empty tomb is not cited in the earlier documents, the belief that the Resurrection was *on the third day* has a place in the earliest known tradition (1 Cor. xv. 4). It is unlikely (and Kirsopp Lake agreed, *op. cit.*, p. 112) that Old Testament passages created this belief. It is far more likely that an event itself created it. For there is the early evidence also that the first day of the week replaced the seventh day because it was the day upon which the Lord rose again (1 Cor. xvi. 2, Acts xx. 7).

III

Of the evidence that has been described different factors have had their special importance for different occasions and needs. To the Apostles themselves it was perhaps the appearances that mattered most. To them the most thrilling fact was that Jesus had shewn Himself to them alive and had spoken with them. This evidence was overwhelming and compelling; and it was more than evidence, it was the risen Jesus Himself. But for subsequent believers the story of the empty tomb would have an increased significance; for it was not enough to

rely upon the testimony of the religious experiences of particular men, and the story of the empty tomb was the clearest
witness to the Act which preceded any and all experiences of
the risen Jesus, to the ἠγέρθη which preceded the ὤφθη.

For centuries the empty tomb became the great evidential
symbol that far more had happened than either the survival of
the soul of Jesus or certain religious experiences of the
Apostles : sin and death had been conquered by the Resurrection of Jesus from out of death. But in modern times the
historical criticism of the Gospels has given rise to the question : was the belief in the empty tomb a false inference and
an unwarranted addition to a primitive Gospel in which
originally it had no place?

CHAPTER IV

History and Criticism

I

FOR many centuries there was little tendency within the
Christian Church to doubt any part of the body of evidence
for the Resurrection which the New Testament contains. The
empty tomb and the appearances both had their place in the
defence and in the interpretation of Christian belief. The
belief was that the body of Jesus was raised from the tomb, not
so as to return to the former mode of life but so as to be
" glorified." It was no longer subject to the laws of its
former existence; it became the perfect instrument of the
spirit. It was—to borrow the phrase by which Paul described
the risen body of the Christians—" raised a spiritual body."

This belief was congruous both with the empty tomb and
with Paul's doctrine of the spiritual body. It was also congruous with two seemingly contrary features in the narratives
of the appearances. On the one hand the narratives describe
Jesus as acting in a manner reminiscent of the conditions of
His life during His earthly ministry. He invites the disciples
to touch Him : He breaks bread and eats with them : He

walks with them. He assures them in all these ways that He is the same Jesus whom they have known before. On the other hand there are features of the narratives which suggest a mode of life new and utterly unlike the former mode. He is seen only by disciples; He is recognised by them gradually; He appears suddenly and as suddenly disappears. These aspects of the story suggest that, if the risen life is indeed bodily, it is bodily with a difference.

Now this twofold aspect of the narratives was taken by orthodox teachers to be evidence of a twofold truth. First, the risen Jesus is the same Jesus, and He enabled the disciples, by the only means that can be imagined, to know that He was the same Jesus whose victory over death had been complete. Yet, though He was the same, He had entered a new mode of being. Into this new mode of being all that had belonged to Him before is taken up and transformed. What previously had been marvellous was now normal, what previously had been normal was now marvellous.

If some theologians, both in the ancient Church and subsequently, took the appearances as manifestations of the risen Body in its essential state, there was another tradition which insisted that the visibility and tangibility by which He made Himself known to the disciples were evidential accommodations made for the disciples' sake. This tradition had celebrated exponents in the ancient Church, notably John Chrysostom in his commentaries. It was upheld by Bishop Westcott: " A little reflection will show that the special outward forms in which the Lord was pleased to make Himself known were no more necessarily connected with His glorified person than the robes which he wore " (*The Gospel of the Resurrection*, p. 112). Yet Westcott was equally firm in his belief that the glorified body was the body that had been raised from the tomb, for " it is not that Christ's soul lives on divested of the essence as of the accidents of the earthly garments in which it was for a time arrayed. It is not that His body, torn and mutilated, is restored such as it was to its former vigour and beauty. But in Him soul and body in the union of a perfect manhood are seen triumphant over the last penalty of sin " (*The Revelation of the Risen Lord*, p. 10).

Westcott's teaching represents the historic faith of the

Church as presented in a spirit of scholarly orthodoxy in the latter decades of the last century. His teaching is of abiding importance. It is in keeping both with the Gospels and with S. Paul. It is, like the work of his master Origen, both profoundly orthodox and strangely modern. It holds to the New Testament belief that the spiritual and the material are not at permanent variance; both are created by God who wills that both shall be redeemed and exalted. It is congruous also with those factors in modern science and philosophy which suggest that the continuity of a body lies not in the identity of the particles which compose it but in the identity of its organization or " form " in relation to the person whose it is. Westcott's teaching may yet be found to outlive the theories which the succeeding half-century has produced.

II

In the past hundred years the evidence for the Resurrection, like every part of the records concerning the origins of Christianity, has been subjected to the methods of historical criticism and research. It had been usual to accept the Gospels as inspired documents of uniform value and authority for the events which they describe; and the task of the historian would be almost limited to attempts to harmonize and to interpret what was recorded. But the application of a rigorous historical science to the Gospels involved the method of treating them " like other books." Their literary sources were unravelled; the tendencies of the different writers or editors were detected; and a frank examination was made of the possibility that the historical material may have been embroidered by legendary elements or by theological motives. In particular the question had to be faced : how far did the early Christians read back developments of doctrine and devotion into their records of the events?

In the case of the Resurrection the scope for such investigations is obviously great. The accounts of the appearances of Jesus are difficult to harmonize into a coherent story. The events of the first Easter morning are difficult to form into a consecutive plan. Above all, is it possible that the Apostles' belief that the *body* of Jesus had been raised from the tomb was a false inference derived from Jewish presuppositions as to what a Resurrection meant, whereas in fact the Resurrection was a survival of the spirit of Jesus? It is around this question that historical research has specially moved.

The attempts of scholars throughout more than a century to discover the real events of Easter, have gone hand in hand with the attempts to discover the real Jesus of history behind the figure described in the New Testament and worshipped by the primitive Church. It is a story full of scholarly achievement, of devotion to Jesus, of zeal for truth. But it is also a story full of the blinding effects of the presuppositions sometimes held by historians who are convinced that they are working without any presuppositions at all. Here it is possible only to record some of the types of conclusions reached by those who have applied the methods of critical science to the narratives of the Resurrection.

(1) First of all there comes into view the line of writers, from Strauss onwards, who have concluded that the appearances of Jesus recorded in the Gospels were simply visions generated by the imaginations of the disciples out of an intense state of emotion or expectancy. In a state of fervent devotion they imagined that they saw Jesus. " Ce qui a ressuscité Jésus, c'est l'amour," wrote Renan in describing how the over-wrought feelings of Mary Magdalene led her to think that she saw her Master. *Strauss* and *Renan* were among the nineteenth-century biographers of Jesus who upheld this " subjective-vision " theory, as it is sometimes called. Among later critical writers who reached this conclusion were *Schmiedel,* whose article on " Resurrection and Ascension narratives " in the *Encyclopedia Biblica* is perhaps the most radical treatment of the problem that has been published, and *Montefiore,* the devout and learned liberal Jew, in his commentary upon the Synoptic Gospels.

It has not been difficult to point out the weaknesses that are involved in this theory. It contradicts some very marked features of the narratives—the slowness of the disciples to grasp that Jesus was alive and to recognize Him, the way in which the appearance so far from reflecting the disciples' own spiritual ideas led them beyond themselves into utterly new and unexpected apprehensions of truth. The theory of course dispenses with the idea of *Resurrection* altogether. Some of those who have held it have combined it with a belief in the immortality of the soul or spirit of Jesus, urging that the disciples should have inferred from the character of their Lord that His life would inevitably continue after death. Their hallucinations thus might serve both to aid and to express their faith in His survival.

(2) There has however been another vision-theory less remote from the main stream of Christian belief. This is the theory of writers who have believed that the residuum of fact behind the narratives consists not in visions generated by the disciples but in visions imparted by God Himself, so as to assure the disciples that Jesus was alive and that His gracious activity was with them in a new and enhanced manner.

This view will long be associated with the name of *Theodor Keim*. In his vast *History of Jesus of Nazara* (1867-1872), the most attractive of the great " liberal " lives of Jesus, Keim criticized the theory of subjective-visions and set forth his belief that God-given visions were granted to the disciples. " We find ourselves in the midst of impossibilities when we make the ordained of God to end, or when we leave the matter to the chance-play of visions, that he is awaked from the dead for the dead. The evidence that Jesus was alive, the *telegram from heaven,* was necessary after an earthly downfall which was unexampled and, in the childhood of the human race, would be convincing. The evidence that he was alive was therefore given by his own impulsion and by the will of God. The Christianity of to-day owes to this evidence, first its Lord and then its own existence : the latter, because it rejoices in him, and because it sees its own future. . . . Thus, though much has fallen away, the faith-fortress of the resurrection of Jesus remains " (English trans., vol. vi, pp. 364-365).

The phrase " telegram from heaven " became well-known as a description of this line of interpretation. Amongst English scholars who have expounded it a special prominence belongs to Dr. Streeter, in his essay in the volume entitled *Foundations* (1910). Streeter believed that the Resurrection of the body of Jesus from the tomb involved intolerable difficulties concerning the nature of the future life, and he interpreted the Resurrection to mean that the spirit of Jesus survived and was able to convey to the disciples the certainty of His presence with them, " possibly showing Himself to them in some form such as might be covered by S. Paul's phrase a ' spiritual body '; possibly through some psychological channel similar to that which explains the mysterious means of communication between persons commonly known as telepathy; or possibly in some way of which we have at present no conception. On such a view the appearances to the disciples can only be called visions, if by visions we mean something directly caused by the Lord Himself, veritably alive and personally in communion with them." Streeter claimed that the Resurrection, thus interpreted, was unique and miraculous and implied an intervention of the power of God altogether beyond our experience. " It is the Lord's doing, and it is marvellous in our eyes." But he believed that the event thus interpreted was nearer to our experience and therefore more credible than the traditional belief that the body was raised and glorified.

But though Streeter, like other exponents of this interpretation, rejected the belief that the body was raised, yet, unlike them, he held that the evidence for the empty tomb was historically convincing. The tomb, he believed, was found empty by the women, not because the body had been raised but because it had been mysteriously removed by human hands. None the less " the discovery of the empty tomb was to some extent a factor in confirming the Apostles in their belief in the Resurrection " (p. 135). It is here that the most difficult feature of Streeter's theory appears. A mistaken inference on the part of the disciples, who ascribed to the power of God what was really an act of unknown human interference with the tomb, was partly the cause of their belief! Here indeed is something hard to believe : that a kind of " providential falsehood " had a place in the revelation of the Resurrection to the disciples and in the historical basis of the Christian faith.

(3) But the interpretation of the Resurrection on these lines as a purely " spiritual " happening has generally been linked with the rejection of the evidence that the body was raised

from the tomb. And here is the crucial point. Many scholars, observing signs of development within the tradition, have maintained that the story of the discovery of the empty grave by the women may be a distorted and fanciful version of what really happened on Easter morning.

Foremost among scholars who reached this conclusion was Dr. Kirsopp Lake. His book, *The Historical Evidence for the Resurrection of Jesus Christ* (1907), is the most thorough of all attempts to trace the growth of the primitive traditions. If it provides the historical student with the most valuable setting out of the main problems, it also throws the most valuable light upon the question of the relation between historical study and doctrinal presuppositions.

Lake's preliminary contention was that the appearances of Jesus were in Galilee and not in Jerusalem. The disciples had fled to Galilee after the Crucifixion. There Jesus appeared to them. On returning to Jerusalem they found that the women were telling a story of how they had visited the tomb of Jesus and found it to be empty. The women's story strengthened the disciples in their belief that Jesus lived, and led them to be sure that there had been a resurrection of His body. The disciples' story in turn encouraged the women in their belief that they had seen the tomb of Jesus empty. But was the story told by the women (cf. Mark xvi. 1-8) a true interpretation of what they saw? We cannot be quite certain. It is possible, Lake contends, that the women visited the wrong grave, and that a young man directed them to the right one: " he is not here : behold the place where they laid him " (the words " he is risen " being an addition to the story). It is possible, Lake goes on, that the women's report was mingled with misunderstanding; and that it all went back to a visit to the wrong grave and an encounter with a stranger which caused them to run away in terror.

Lake therefore would reject the historicity of the empty tomb. But towards the close of his discussion he makes a very important observation :

" The historical evidence is such that it can be fairly interpreted consistently with either of the two doctrinal positions . . . but it does not support either. The story of the empty tomb must be fought out on doctrinal, not on historical or critical grounds " (p. 253).

The evidence, Lake tells us, is inconclusive : our decision will rest upon our doctrinal prejudice. It depends upon whether our view of the future life is " the resurrection of a material body " or " the unbroken survival of personal life." Upon this our interpretation of the historical question will rest. Lake himself believes in " the unbroken survival of personal life," and his decision about the Resurrection of Christ accords with his presupposition.

These words of Lake are of the utmost significance. The author of the most scientific treatment of the historical problem that has been written, in this and perhaps in any language, admits in the end that a decision cannot be made without recourse to religious presupposition.

III

From this sketch of some of the chief theories which have arisen in the historical study of the evidence for the Resurrection one certainty at least emerges : the investigation of the historical problem has again and again been interwoven with doctrinal and philosophical considerations. Sometimes the presence of presuppositions, whether traditional or modern, is acknowledged, as Kirsopp Lake has shewn us. But often writers about Jesus Christ have claimed to be conducting a purely historical investigation in strict impartiality; and yet decisive, though unconscious, presuppositions have been present. Too often writers of the school which has been most certain of its freedom from presuppositions have been slow to examine and to criticize the presuppositions which they have employed :

For the whole question of presuppositions is an exceedingly difficult one. It would seem to be the greatest gain when historians can eschew the presuppositions derived from ancient orthodoxy and can investigate the origins of Christianity in a spirit of detached and impartial inquiry. Yet the avowal of a historian that he is working without presuppositions has so often, in the field of New Testament study, opened the way to the dominance of new presuppositions. Indeed history without presuppositions is impossible : a historian must needs bring to his task a certain view of the world and a certain mental furniture of his own. The historian of Jesus Christ, confronted with unique occurrences in the documents, may explain them in the light of presuppositions derived from a belief in the uniqueness of Jesus Christ in relation to a redemption—and perhaps a supernatural and cosmic redemption —wrought through Him by God. Or he may explain them away in the light of presuppositions which demand that Jesus Christ be fitted into certain naturalistic beliefs about the world, man and religion. Or he may employ a variety of other presuppositions. But what does not exist is a historical procedure wherein presuppositions have no place at all.

Now in the study of the Resurrection certain presuppositions have occurred. Here is an illustration of them, in a commentary on St. Luke's Gospel where the historical questions are discussed :

> "The modern mind cannot accept the idea of a bodily resurrection for humanity. The future life is viewed as a spiritual, not as a physical existence; in which personality, not the physical organism survives. Apart therefore from the question of the miraculous, the story of the empty tomb seems unnecessary, inconsequent, even crude; in Lake's words 'an improper inference from the fact of the Resurrection.'" (H. K. Luce, *S. Luke*, p. 366.)

Here indeed are some highly questionable propositions. It is not clear that the "modern mind," as exemplified in science and philosophy, is in sympathy with the sharp antithesis between "personality" and "physical organism." Nor is it clear that what happens for "mankind" in general must determine what should fittingly happen for Jesus Christ, for may not the Resurrection have been not a typical survival to illustrate the fact that all good men survive but a unique redemptive act whereby death was conquered for our sake?

It seems that three presuppositions are here apparent, and they have indeed often been adopted. (1) The one notion is that the body has no place in man's future life. Into this notion the interpretation of our Lord's Resurrection must be fitted. (2) The second notion is that the human race is destined for a spiritual immortality through the survival of the soul after death. Into this notion Jesus Christ as a member of the human race must be fitted. Neither of these notions is peculiarly modern, and it needs demonstration that the most modern science or philosophy tends to support them. These two notions are used in conjunction with a third. (3) This is the notion that the Resurrection of Jesus is not, as the Apostles taught, the unique spring and source of our resurrection but rather an exemplary edifying symbol of our survival after death. What is normal for righteous men is thus the norm of the Resurrection of Jesus.

It is here that the real distinction lies. The real issue is not between a " bodily " and a " spiritual " event : for the orthodox may err in clinging to the inadequate word " bodily " as greatly as the modernist may err in clinging to the inadequate word " spiritual." The issue is rather between two different beliefs about the Gospel. According to the one belief Jesus Christ is interpreted within the series of evolution and history in such a way that the transcendental and redemptive aspects of the Gospel receive less than their proper place : the Resurrection is an example to us that if we are good we may, like Jesus, survive death. According to the other belief the Resurrection is a divine intervention, transcendent and creative, whereby a new creation is inaugurated in the life of mankind and the world. For such a Gospel the story of the empty tomb can never be " unnecessary, inconsequent, even crude."

Now it would be unfair to say that the interpretation of the Resurrection, along the lines of Keim or Streeter, as an exaltation of the spirit of Jesus, necessarily misses the transcendental and redemptive meaning of the Gospel. Such an interpretation *may* conserve the uniqueness of the event as more than a survival. As its most recent exponent has urged : " It is sometimes said that mere visions of Jesus, even if objective, might establish the fact that he had survived death, but not that he had conquered it. But if Jesus survived death in such a sort as to be able to energize and inspire his disciples, he *had* conquered it; nor would the resuscitation of

his material body make the conquest more real or glorious"
(C. J. Cadoux, *The Historic Mission of Jesus*, 1941, p. 282).
True, to think thus of the Resurrection does not inevitably
imply a departure from a belief in its uniqueness and its
redemptive character. None the less two things can be said.
(1) It is hard to see how the Apostles or their converts could
have been convinced of a redemptive victory over death by
Jesus had they believed that His body was corrupted in the
grave. (2) The view of a spiritual survival of Jesus held by
a long line of scholars has been frankly linked with the presuppositions that we have described. These presuppositions
have often been decisive in the handling of the evidence about
the tomb. The criticism which rejects the empty tomb as *a
priori* incredible or inconsequent or crude has its roots in a
philosophy which is far removed from the New Testament.
For the Gospel in the New Testament involves the freedom of
the living God and an act of new creation which includes the
bodily no less than the spiritual life of man.

IV

It is with history that we are concerned. What happened?
That is what Christians desire to know. In seeking the answer
there is need for the most scientific approach to historical
truth that is possible.

But the era of historical criticism has disclosed faults of
method which it is now possible to detect. It was a great gain
when liberal theology linked the belief in Creation to the facts
of the evolution of nature and man, and so enabled us to
study afresh the divine action in the processes of nature and in
the gradual movement of history. But it was the fault of
liberal theology sometimes to go far towards eliminating the
other aspect of the divine action, namely the unique and
transcendental work of God whose redemption is a breaking
into history from above. This fault in theological thinking
begat presuppositions fatal to the handling of the history of
Jesus.

Now it would be none the less fatal for us to go behind
the methods of historical criticism and to rest in doctrinal

affirmations. *Non tali auxilio.* In connection with the Resurrection narratives no difficulty must be ignored; and the possibility must be faced that, here as elsewhere, unreliable and legendary elements may have found their way into the traditions and the documents. The technique of literary and historical criticism, the analysis of sources and of the work of editors, must be employed to the full.

But to discard presuppositions altogether would be an impossible adventure; and rather than claim to discard presuppositions the present writer would ask sympathy for two very modest presuppositions. The one is that the Biblical belief in the living God, creator, redeemer, transcendent, is true. The other is that the events must be such as account for the Gospel which the Apostles preached and by which the first Christians lived. We would not use these presuppositions for the pressing of historical conclusions; but we would so bear them in mind as to avoid a sort of inhibition if the converging lines of evidence seem to point to a supernatural event at the climax of the story of Christ. Thus if the evidence is pointing us towards a Resurrection of an utterly unique sort we will not be incredulous, for the Christ is Himself a unique and transcendent fact in history. If the evidence is pointing us towards a miracle we will not be troubled, for the miracle will mean not only a breach of the laws that have been perceived in this world but a manifestation of the purpose of the creator of a new world and the redeemer of our own. And if the evidence is pointing us towards an act wherein spirit and body are strangely blended and exalted, our minds will have no terrors: for the message of the New Testament is pervaded through and through by the belief that the spiritual and the material are interwoven in the purpose of the Word-made-flesh. Why is it judged incredible with you, if God should raise the dead?

CHAPTER V

The Evidence of the Gospels

The Nature of the Problem

THE narratives of the Resurrection present a number of difficult questions, and it is important that in studying them we should see where the problem really lies. The scholars of an older generation were concerned to construct, if possible, a harmony of the events recorded by the four Evangelists; and the credibility of the records has often been thought to depend upon the possibility of such a harmony being made. To-day, new knowledge of the character and composition of the Gospels seems to shew that such a harmony is not to be expected, and that the absence of it need not impugn the historical worth of the traditions which the Gospels contain. The task is rather to discover the primitive traditions that lie behind the narratives, to detect the ways in which these traditions may have been developed or corrupted, and to trace the methods and motives with which the evangelists have woven the traditions into frameworks of their own.

The process behind the making of the Gospels falls into several stages. (1) There was first the oral tradition of the deeds and words of Jesus, handed down by Christian teachers through several decades. Stories would be told in the Christian communities of the things which Jesus had taught and done. Inevitably the stories would be strung together not necessarily in chronological or biographical order, but in shapes or plans suitable for the purposes of teaching about the various themes of the Gospel. Inevitably also there would be embellishments made in the stories during this process of oral tradition. (2) There was finally the work of the evangelists who took the traditions that had come down to them, now partly in written sources as well as in oral form, and moulded these traditions into continuous narratives of the events of the Gospel. Here too we can detect embellishments made by different evangelists as editors, and we can trace the special tendencies of each evangelist as he edits the traditions into his own framework. As often as not the framework may be arbitrary, and we cannot harmonize the frameworks of the evangelists one with another. Yet all these facts do not lead us to doubt that the Gospels preserve for us true accounts of the deeds and sayings of Jesus. For we can sometimes see in the material a primitive perspective that takes us behind the developments in the theology of the Apostolic age. We can trace the primitive themes of the words and deeds of Jesus as recorded in several distinct "blocks" of tradition. And we can compare these results with our other evidence concerning the Gospel which the Apostles preached in the earliest days.

Now the Resurrection narratives seem to have been built up in much the same way as the other narratives in the Gospels; and the problems are not dissimilar. We can detect some of the early stories by which the message of the Resurrection would be told. We can perceive certain embellishments in the growth of the tradition. We can perceive also the tendencies and motives of the evangelists as they edit the material into their own frames. But between the Resurrection narratives and the other Gospel narratives there are two significant differences. (1) Inevitably there is a special difficulty in the order and geographical plan of the stories. From the very nature of the case we would expect it to be difficult for the Christian teachers to conserve order and plan in their stories of the appearances of the risen Jesus to groups of people at different places and times. (2) On the other hand the story of the Resurrection was, together with the story of the Passion, a central part of the teaching of the Apostles from the beginning. It was part of the core of the Gospel. If therefore there are embellishments we remember also that the stories would be handed down with a very special regard for the testimony of eye-witnesses and the authority of Apostles.

The Traditions behind the Narratives

As we read the narratives we can observe within them some of the forms of story-telling which were used by the early teachers of the Resurrection.[1] There is the brief sentence telling the good news : " The Lord is risen indeed, and hath appeared to Simon " (Luke xxiv. 34). There is the story that tells of an appearance of Jesus, told vividly so as to make it plain that Jesus truly was seen and that no mistake was made; an instance is the story of how Jesus shewed His hands and His feet to the disciples and ate a piece of broiled fish before them (Luke xxiv. 36-43). There were also stories telling of the bewilderment and dejection of the disciples and of the way in which it gradually came home to them that Jesus was alive; an instance is the story of the walk to Emmaus (Luke xxiv. 13-35). There were also stories of the teaching given by the risen Jesus, told so as to shew the purpose of the Resurrection and its lessons for the disciples then and for the members of the Church in days to come (cf. Matt. xxviii. 16-20, Luke xxiv. 44-49, John xxi. 1-14). There was also the story of the visit of the women to the tomb and their discovery that it was empty (Mark xvi. 1-8). In all these ways the early Christian teachers would hand down the message of the Resurrection.

These stories, at first told orally, are now known to us through their presence in the narratives of the Gospels. Two questions arise : What signs of embellishment in the traditions are noticeable? What signs are there on the other hand that a genuinely primitive perspective has been retained?

(1) The possibilities of embellishment in the tradition will be apparent at once to a reader who will examine in turn the accounts of the visit of the women to the tomb in Mark and in Matthew. In Mark the miracle is implied but not described. The story is told in utter simplicity. The women arrive wondering who will move the stone so that they may

[1] This subject has been examined afresh in the interesting essay by C. H. Dodd on " The Appearances of the Risen Christ: an essay in Form-Criticism of the Gospels " in the volume *Studies in the Gospels* edited by D. E. Nineham.

enter. They see that the stone is no longer there. They enter. The tomb is empty. A young man in a white robe tells them that Jesus is not there, and bids them tell the disciples that He will go before them into Galilee. They flee in fear, and tell no one. The reticence of the story tells us of the great event which has come to pass. How great a contrast is seen in Matthew's narrative. In place of the quiet implication of a miracle there is an elaborate description. There was a great earthquake; an angel of the Lord descended and rolled away the stone; his appearance was like lightning, and the soldiers on guard trembled and became as dead men. Such is an editor's embroidery of his source; and if elaboration of the tradition took place in the written stage it is reasonable to think that it took place in the oral stage too.

Other illustrations could be given of the ways in which the traditions became modified in the decades between the events themselves and the writing of the several Gospels. It would be possible for details or sayings connected with one story to be transferred to another story, or for the geographical setting of a story to become confused. Interesting elaborations of the tradition are noticeable in the descriptions of the burial of Jesus and of the character of Joseph of Arimathaea; we can trace in the Gospels a growing tendency to dwell upon the discipleship of Joseph and to treat him as one who is within the true fold. There is also a narrative in which many of the most conservative scholars have been ready to admit the likelihood of a legendary element. This is the story of the guard at the tomb in Matthew xxvii. 62-66, xxviii. 11-15: it contains a number of distinct improbabilities, and it is akin to a cycle of stories used (though not often) by Matthew, which arouse a suspicion that they present Christian *midrash* rather than history.

(2) Yet the presence of embellishments such as these makes it all the more impressive that the stories retain so many signs of a truly primitive perspective.

In his work *Die Formgeschichte des Evangeliums,* a searching examination of the growth of the traditions behind the Gospels, Dr. Martin Dibelius expressed the view that the Emmaus story " has been preserved in an almost pure form," and that the story of the visit of the women to the tomb is in

Mark's version "in its pure form," except for the message about Galilee which he regards as an insertion made so as to link the story with other stories.[1] This judgment is not surprising. Both these stories give the impression that they are taking us behind the formal apologetic of the Church and are shewing us the original bewilderment and half-awareness of the disciples and of the women. In both of these stories there is the atmosphere less of demonstration and proof than of the growing awareness of a miracle unexpected and hard to comprehend. There could scarcely be less of the conventional methods of miracle-story-telling: the disciples are made aware of the great event only as Jesus reveals Himself to them in the Scriptures, in personal converse and finally in the breaking of the bread. It is important also to notice the allusions within the Emmaus story to other parts of the traditions, to an appearance to Peter (Luke xxiv. 34) and to the news brought by the women (xxiv. 22-24), allusions made in a manner so different from that of the narrator of evidence who is striving to prove his case.

Such are the traditions that we find behind the narratives in the Gospels. Some of them are embellished, and some are strikingly undeveloped. That we should expect to be able to weave the stories into a chronological and geographical plan seems inconceivable. But if we eschew the quest for an external unity between the stories, we can the more perceive the inward unity that belongs to them. They are, with very few exceptions, at one in the *manner* of their testimony; and this is a manner which it is very hard to attribute to anything else except the spiritually subtle nature of the event itself. They are at one in that which they affirm, both by cross-reference and by direct description: the appearance of Jesus and the discovery of the empty tomb. Moreover they are at one also with the primitive Apostolic preaching that Christ was buried and was raised again on the third day, and with the primitive revolution whereby the first day of the week replaced the sabbath as "the day which the Lord hath made."

[1] English translation (1934 edition), pp. 190 ff.

The Framework of the Evangelists

Each evangelist draws upon the traditions which he knows, and builds the stories into a framework in accordance with his own special purpose.

In the case of *Mark* the true text, as we now possess it, ends at xvi. 8:

" And they went out, and fled from the tomb; for trembling and astonishment had come upon them; and they said nothing to anyone; for they were afraid."[1]

It has been the widespread opinion of modern scholars (including Hort, Swete and Burkitt) that this verse cannot be the point at which Mark intended to conclude his Gospel; that the book was mutilated at a very early date; that there existed a concluding section which is now lost; and that this section very likely included an account of an appearance of Jesus to Peter in Galilee in fulfilment of the message from the tomb. (It is thought unlikely that Matthew made use of the lost ending of Mark; but a possible connection has been suggested between the lost ending of Mark and the fishing scene in Galilee recorded in John xxi. and the description in the Apocryphal " Gospel of Peter " of the disciples returning to Galilee after the Passion to resume their former work.) The general trend of modern commentators has been to deny that these words can possibly be the deliberate ending to a sentence, a story, or a Gospel.

On the other hand some powerful arguments from recent writers have to be reckoned with, on the side of the view that Mark may really have planned to end his Gospel just at this very point. Literary parallels have been found to shew the possibility of sentences that end with γὰρ. It is also pointed out that the abruptness is in keeping with Mark's style of

[1] The section " Mark " xvi. 9-20, familiar as the conclusion of the Gospel in Authorized Version and Revised Version, is now generally recognized not to be Mark's work but an early compilation, written so as to make the story more complete. The contrast in style between this section and Mark's own narrative is obvious; and the section fits the preceding story very clumsily.

writing. Throughout his Gospel he has recorded the awe and bewilderment caused by the words and deeds of the Son of God. What would be more characteristic of him than to end his story by telling of the awe and bewilderment caused by the news that Christ was risen? The women were seeking Jesus the Nazarene, the dead body of the Crucified : but, says the voice at the tomb, the disciples will see Him, glorified, in Galilee. That is the end. What more should Mark say? for by his reticence he tells us so much of the indescribable mystery of the Resurrection.[1]

If probability still lies with the view that there is a " lost ending," the view that the true ending is at the words " for they were afraid " deserves more consideration than it usually receives. But if there be a " lost ending " we cannot infer with any certainty what it contained. It is idle to affirm that it *must* have contained this or that story. As we shall see, the deductions sometimes drawn from the message to the disciples are most hazardous.

Matthew (i.) follows Mark in his account of the empty tomb, with a good deal of editorial embroidery (xviii. 1-7). (ii.) He adds the story of the soldiers guarding the tomb (xxvii. 62-66, xviii. 11-15) in the interests of apologetic against a slander that the disciples stole the body. (iii.) He inserts a brief section to tell of the movements of the women from the point where Mark's abrupt ending leaves them. They recovered from their panic and went on their way to tell the disciples : Jesus appeared to them, and they worshipped Him (xxviii. 8-10). (iv.) Then Matthew concludes with a scene in Galilee. Here Jesus appears to the eleven, and apparently to other disciples, at a mountain which the Lord appointed; and He gives a final missionary charge (xxviii. 16-20). Matthew records no appearances to the disciples in Jerusalem. Here, as elsewhere, the only historical frame that he possesses is that which Mark provides; and Mark here provides less than he might have wished. But Matthew has all that he needs for the climax of his own Gospel. The

---

[1] The view that Mark intended to end at xvi. 8 is set forth by J. M. Creed in *Journal of Theological Studies*, January 1930, and by R. H. Lightfoot in *The Gospel Message of St. Mark* ch. vii. On the other side see W. L. Knox in *Harvard Theological Review*, January 1942.

royal Messiah, claiming all authority in heaven and on earth, once more teaches His disciples with authority upon a Mount. He commissions them as Apostles in a universal Church that replaces the old Israel, and He promises that His presence will be with them unto the end of the age.

Luke also follows Mark in his story of the empty tomb (xxiv. 1-7) with however a number of interesting divergences. These divergences may be due to the use of another source besides Mark. But the most important divergence seems to be due to editing. In place of the message of the young man :

"Go, tell his disciples and Peter, He goeth before you into Galilee; there shall ye see him, as he said unto you."

Luke records these words

"Remember how he spake unto you, when he was yet in Galilee, saying that the Son of Man must be delivered up into the hands of sinful men, and be crucified, and the third day rise again."

No doubt Luke edited the message in this way on account of the fact that he did not intend to record appearances in Galilee; though some would urge that Luke was preserving another tradition about the form of the message.

Luke's subsequent narratives are all peculiar to his Gospel, and the events are set in and near Jerusalem. (i.) First, *some* of the women who were at the tomb bring the news to the eleven and to all the rest; but the news seems to the disciples to be idle talk (xxiv. 8-11). (ii.) Then, according to some MSS., Peter visits the tomb to confirm the news for himself (xxiv. 12, omitted by Codex Bezae). (iii.) There follows the Emmaus story, perhaps the most beautiful and arresting of them all. Jesus joins on the road from Jerusalem two dejected disciples who have heard of the story of the women but have learnt nothing that convinces them of the Resurrection. Unrecognized, Jesus unfolds to them the Scriptures concerning the necessity of the Cross and the Resurrection. The walk ends at Emmaus, where Jesus is recognized when he blesses and breaks bread with the two disciples : but as soon as He is recognized, He disappears. The two disciples return at once to Jerusalem and find the eleven who are saying " The Lord is risen indeed, and hath appeared to Simon " (xxiv. 13-35).[1] (iv.) Then Luke records an appearance of Jesus to the disciples, then and there assembled on Easter evening. He invites them to touch Him, and He eats in their presence (xxiv. 36-43). (v.) A discourse follows, concerning the fulfilment of prophecy, the mission of the Church and the coming gift of power from on high (xxiv. 44-49). (vi.) Finally, Jesus leads the disciples over against Bethany, blesses them and is parted from them. (The more probable text says simply " he was parted," ἀπέστη : a doubtful text includes the words " and was carried up into heaven," ἀνεήφθη. It is in Acts that the one explicit description of the Ascension occurs : " he was taken up, and a cloud received him out of their sight," Acts i. 9.)

Luke records no appearances in Galilee; and on a first impression his narrative suggests that there was no room for any visit of the disciples to Galilee. Event *seems* to follow event in rapid succession from the walk to Emmaus to the parting at Bethany. But (1) vagueness in chronology is one of Luke's characteristics as a writer; and we do not know that he means the contents of his last chapter to be in a direct and rapid sequence. If he does mean it to be so, then the parting would take place late at night, which seems improbable. May there not be a break before the discourse at verse 44, or before the walk towards Bethany at verse 50? (2) In the opening verses of Acts Luke seems to correct any impression he may have left that the events all happened on the one day, for he tells us that the period of the appearances lasted " during forty days." It is wrong therefore to infer that Luke's narrative excludes the possibility that there were, in fact, appearances in Galilee. Nor is Luke's own omission of any Galilean tradition difficult to explain. It is upon Jerusalem that his thoughts are centred. His theme is the going-up of Jesus to Jerusalem to die, the redemption wrought in Jeru-

[1] There is a noteworthy variant reading in Luke xxiv. 34, λεγόντες for λεγόντας, which ascribes the words " The Lord is risen indeed . . ." not to the eleven but to the two who had come from Emmaus.

salem, the continuity of the divine purpose through the events in Jerusalem, the mission of the Church from Jerusalem, the advance of the Gospel from Jerusalem to Rome. That is Luke's theme; he is absorbed in it; he telescopes his story in accordance with it; he omits what would be a diversion from it.

John is at pains to blend together factors in the tradition—both historical and doctrinal—which hitherto have been presented somewhat apart. Historically, he shews that there was a link between the evidence of the women at the tomb and the evidence of the Apostles in Jerusalem—namely the visit of Peter and John to the tomb to verify the women's story. He shews also that he knows and values traditions both of Jerusalem and of Galilee. Doctrinally, he shews how great is the importance both of the mysterious and of the bodily aspects of the Resurrection of Jesus. He blends the vivid evidence of sight and touch with contrary lessons on believing without touch (xx. 17) and without sight (xx. 29).

His narrative begins with a visit not of a group of women but of Mary Magdalene alone to the tomb. It was dark. She found the tomb empty, and told the disciples (xx. 1-2). There follows the visit of Peter and John to the tomb to confirm the news (xx. 3-10). Meanwhile Jesus appears to Mary Magdalene by the tomb and gives her the command not to cling to Him but to go and tell the disciples that He is ascending to the Father (xx. 11-18). On the same day at evening Jesus appears to the eleven in Jerusalem, shews them His hands and His side, bestows the gift of Holy Spirit upon them and sends them forth even as the Father sent Him (xx. 19-23). A week later there comes the episode of doubting Thomas (xx. 24-29), and some words which sum up the purpose of the Gospel. An Epilogue follows (possibly from another hand) to tell of an appearance of Jesus to some of the disciples fishing in Galilee (xxi.).

In all this John is drawing out a theological interpretation of the Resurrection. In the next chapter of this book the reader will be asked to study this theological interpretation, and to notice how John shews the relation between the Resurrection stories and the great themes of his Gospel. But John is no less concerned to emphasize the importance of history; and if the new material which he introduces is in some ways hard to harmonize with the earlier accounts, in other ways it corroborates their story and supplies some convincing links to it. John's story of Mary Magdalene is not incompatible with Mark's story of the women as a group. John's story of Peter and John running to the tomb confirms hints given in the Emmaus story of Luke. John's story of the appearance to the eleven confirms both Luke and Paul. The epilogue confirms a Galilean tradition.

Such are the ways in which the four evangelists build the traditions which they use into the frameworks which we know. The plan and purpose of each is intelligible, both in what he includes and in what he omits. It is a fascinating study to attempt to harmonize what the evangelists tell us and to essay a reconstruction of the events in an ordered scheme of time and place. Up to a point the attempt may be successful, but a limit to the success is always reached. That this is so need not disturb us, for the right question for the historian who is aware of the nature of the Gospels and their composition is not, Can a harmony be constructed? How utterly suspicious we ought to be, if here alone in the whole range of the Gospel narratives, a neat harmony could be provided! No: the right questions are: Can we account for the plan adopted by each evangelist? Do the narratives include primitive traditions? Do these traditions concur with one another in their testimony to the main event? Are these traditions corroborated by our other evidence about the primitive preaching of the Apostles? It does not seem to be too confident for us to affirm that the answer to each of the questions is, yes.

Galilee and Jerusalem

It would none the less be disturbing if the narratives included a discrepancy so great as to impugn their credibility. What then of the biggest discrepancy that has been alleged— the conflict between the tradition of an appearance in Galilee found in Matthew and the tradition of appearances in Jerusalem found in Luke? This problem has been regarded as a central crux.

The Galilean tradition has had some firm adherents, who have believed it to be the earliest and the best and the key to the understanding of the whole development of the traditions concerning the Resurrection. Dr. Lake in *The Historical Evidence of the Resurrection of Jesus Christ* (1907) and Mr. Gardner-Smith in *The Narratives of the Resurrection* (1926) have presented this view on the basis of the most thorough attempts to unravel the traditions.

Why Galilee? (i.) It is urged that Mark, our earliest document, clearly points towards an appearance in Galilee as the climax of its own story. No other climax, it is said, could have been intended after the message xvi. 7 : " He goeth before you into Galilee." (ii.) Then it is urged that the disciples were in Galilee already. Lake argued that they had fled away home at the time of the Crucifixion and had sought their former way of life, disillusioned (an extreme inference from Mark xiv. 50, " they all left him, and fled "). Gardner-Smith criticized this view, pointed out that it is unlikely that the disciples would have left the city during the feast, and pre-ferred a tradition found in the Apocryphal " Gospel of Peter " : that the disciples fled back to Galilee only when the feast was over. This Apocryphal work is no doubt gnostic, tendentious and unreliable, but it may none the less preserve portions of early traditions. For after a passage describing the visit of the women to the tomb (a passage which draws freely upon the Marcan and Matthaean records or traditions) " pseudo-Peter " continues :

" Now it was the last day of unleavened bread, and many went out returning to their homes since the feast was over. But we, the twelve disciples of the Lord, were weeping and grieving : and each one, mourning for that which was come to pass, departed to his own home. But I, Simon Peter, and Andrew my brother took our nets and went away to the sea. And Levi, the son of Alphaeus was with us, whom the Lord . . ." (The rest is lost.)

Here is a story of the return of the disciples to Galilee and to their old life. Lake held that it is based upon the lost end of Mark, Gardner-Smith that it is based rather upon the cycle of traditions from which the lost end of Mark arose. It fits the picture presented by the fishing-scene in John xxi. " Can there be any other explanation than that he is following an earlier tradition which the other evangelists have deserted?" (iii.) There is indeed a further plea for the Galilean tradition. It is far easier to explain how stories of appearances in Galilee might come to be transferred to Jerusalem, the subsequent centre of the Church, than it is to explain how the Galilean tradition arose if the appearances were in Jerusalem.

So speak the " Galileans." In their view the disciples were in Galilee, and Jesus appeared to them there. They subsequently returned to Jerusalem (where *later* appearances may have occurred). Then a tradition grew which transposed to Jerusalem the stories of the first appearances, partly perhaps with the motive of bringing the evidence of the disciples into closer proximity with the story of the women at the tomb, and partly because Jerusalem had become the centre of the life of the Church. As we have seen, a chief corollary of the Galilean theory is that there is a gap between the disciples and the women, and the women's testimony could not be verified by the disciples.

But the Galilean theory is vulnerable. It demands an extreme scepticism concerning the traditions which Luke records, especially the Emmaus story with its naïve and seemingly primitive cross-references to the traditions about Peter and the women. It called forth the alternative hypothesis of Dr. Burkitt, that Peter set out for Galilee on receiving the message from the tomb, but Jesus appeared to him on his journey and bade him return to Jerusalem. But the real weakness of the theory is that it rests primarily upon a conjecture as to the contents of the lost ending of Mark, and it is utterly hazardous to affirm what this lost ending *must* have contained. It is not certain that the message at the tomb necessarily demands a first appearance in Galilee as its sequel. The message recalls the words of Jesus before the Passion :

" All ye shall be offended : for it is written, I will smite the shepherd and the sheep shall be scattered abroad. Howbeit, after I am raised up, I will go before you into Galilee." (Mark xiv. 27-28.)

The imagery is that of a shepherd. Jesus had led the disciples from Galilee to Jerusalem, προάγων, "going before them" (x. 32). And after the Resurrection he will go before them like a shepherd once more, leading them into Galilee. Thus the message at the tomb,

"He goeth before you into Galilee,"

may well mean not that Jesus will forestall the disciples there, but that He will direct them thither from another place. An appearance first in Jerusalem is not excluded. How indeed were the women to deliver the message to the disciples unless they were near at hand in Jerusalem?

It is probable that the Galilean theory, in its extreme form, will go the way of many theories that have for a time dominated the discussion of historical problems. It is noteworthy that its chief supporter came to admit a faltering in his allegiance to it. In his latest writing on the subject (*The Beginnings of Christianity,* vol. v., 1933) Lake shewed far less confidence. " More or less corrupted forms of such a tradition are to be found in Matt. xxviii. 16-20, in John xxi. and in the Gospel of Peter. They are, relatively speaking, unimportant; the theory of a Galilean tradition really stands or falls with the interpretation of Mark xiv. 28 and xvi. 7 " (p. 8). " Thus though Professor Burkitt's suggestion seems at least sufficiently attractive to make me waver in my allegiance to the Galilean hypothesis, I am not wholly convinced that he is right " (p. 14).

For are we faced simply with the neat alternative : Galilee *or* Jerusalem? Is it not reasonable to suppose that there may have been appearances in both localities? It may well be that, whereas Luke is right in describing an appearance to the eleven in Jerusalem on Easter Day and in taking Jerusalem to be the main centre, there were also appearances in Galilee. Perhaps others in Galilee besides the eleven were permitted to see Jesus (cf. " the five hundred brethren " mentioned by Paul); perhaps Jesus directed the eleven thither for the purpose of an appearance vocational in its object and linked with the mission to the Gentiles.[1]

It seems, finally, to be the greatest mistake to take the record of the message at the tomb as a kind of clue to the course of events and a key to the reconstruction of the story. It is astonishing that scholars have built so much upon these words; for they seem to be the very point in the tradition where certainty is least possible to attain. Who spoke the words? What exactly did they mean? What does the evangelist understand them to mean? These are the last questions about which we can ever speak with sure knowledge. Perhaps the message about Galilee, and the saying of Jesus before the Passion to which it looks back, had a meaning symbolical rather than geographical and referred less to a place of meeting or journeying than to a Victory and a Mission that would follow the disaster of the Cross. Who knows?

The Tomb

To the empty tomb witness is borne by the narrative of Mark, by references within the Emmaus story in Luke, and by the tradition in John. It is possible that John's story of the visit of Mary Magdalene goes back to a tradition as early as the tradition about the women recorded in Mark. It is certain that we have the testimony of the earliest Gospel, and of cross-references in a Lucan tradition. Are traditions, thus attested in the Gospels and congruous with the primitive preaching, to be discredited, apart from *a priori* considerations?

The scope for scepticism about Mark's story is enlarged if the Galilean theory be held. For the theory creates a gap between the experiences of the women at the tomb and the experiences of the disciples who saw Jesus, and—Lake contended—gives room for the possibility that the women's story, unchecked by the disciples, contained misunderstanding of what really happened. Perhaps they went to the wrong tomb,

[1] For the symbolism of Galilee in connection with the Gentiles see pp. 77-78 and C. F. Evans on " I will go before you into Galilee " in *Journal of Theological Studies,* April 1954.

and a young man directed them to the right one, saying " He is not here, behold the place where they laid him " or (as Codex Bezae has it) " behold there his place," ἴδετε ἐκεῖ τόπον αὐτοῦ. Thus a terrifying experience and a misunderstanding formed the basis of the Marcan story.

This hypothesis depends to a considerable extent upon the Galilean theory, which invites—as we have seen—many doubts. It depends also upon a rejection of the evidence that the disciples verified the women's report. Is it conceivable that the disciples would have heard of the empty tomb without going to see for themselves? And is it conceivable that they could have preached that Jesus " was buried and was raised again " without any interest in the grave?

Apart from scepticism about Mark's account (a scepticism in which, as Lake himself has said, presuppositions have a decisive place) there remains the question why no evidence for the empty tomb is cited in the documents earlier than the Gospels. (1) As regards Paul's omission in 1 Corinthians xv., Lake has supplied an answer : " Was there any reason why S. Paul should have supplied these details had he known them? Surely not. He was not trying to convince the Corinthians that the Lord was risen : he was reminding them that he had already convinced them." (ii.) As regards the accounts that we possess of the primitive Gospel in the Epistles and the Acts, the omission of references to the evidence about the tomb is *intelligible*. The accounts are brief, and dwell upon the Gospel itself rather than upon the apologetic evidence used to support it. The Gospel was that Christ died, was buried, was raised and appeared; it implies the empty tomb. But the most prominent part of the evidence was the appearances : for it was the appearances that brought to the Apostles not only evidence but more than evidence in the thrilling consciousness of Christ Himself, glorified and victorious.

" He appeared to Cephas, then to the twelve. . . ."

Those were the experiences that mattered intensely to the Apostles, as evidence and as far more. But for the generations to come there was need for greater recourse to that part of the evidence that was not bound up with the particular experiences of the disciples and that spoke plainly of the event that lay behind. It is this evidence which the evangelists set out when they include the narratives of the empty tomb; and in so doing they make complete for all time their witness to the Gospel :

"how that Christ *died* for our sins according to the scriptures :
and that he was *buried*;
and that he hath been *raised* on the third day according to the scriptures :
and that he *appeared*. . . ."

CHAPTER VI

The Theology of the Gospel Narratives

THE study of the historical problems presented by the narratives of the Resurrection ought never to be separated from the study of the theological themes of the narratives. For the narratives are the climax of four books written so as to present the Gospel of God. Each evangelist has his own emphasis upon certain aspects of the Gospel and his own way of expressing them; and the themes prominent in the stories of the Resurrection are bound up with the themes of each Gospel as a whole. Just as each evangelist has his own angle of approach to the " Gospel of Jesus Christ the Son of God," so each has his own special insight into the message that " Christ was raised again on the third day according to the Scriptures."

Mark

We have already noticed the probability that the true conclusion of Mark's Gospel is lost. But it is unfortunate that preoccupation with the fragmentariness of Mark's present ending has sometimes blinded us to the great theological significance of what does survive. Mark xvi. 1-8, the story of the coming of the women to the tomb, is a story in itself, such as might be told in the oral teaching of the early Christians. Its profound teaching is the climax of the recurring themes of the book.

The breathless abruptness of these verses is in keeping with a breathless abruptness which appears again and again in the Marcan Gospel. Abruptly, without preparation or introduction or note of date or background, the story begins : " The beginning of the Gospel of Jesus Christ the Son of God . . . was John who baptized in the wilderness and preached the baptism of repentance unto the remission of sins." God is intervening in history; his Reign is breaking into the world. Presently the preaching of Jesus has begun : " The time is fulfilled, and the kingdom of God is at hand : repent ye, and believe in the Gospel." The event is bewildering. The note of bewilderment recurs. The words and deeds of Jesus seem to lead the disciples from perplexity to perplexity. " They were amazed." " They became sore afraid." " They understood not the saying and were afraid to ask him." " And they were in the way going up to Jerusalem; and Jesus was going before them : and they were amazed; and they that followed were afraid." " All ye shall be offended." The words with which the present concluding section ends are in keeping with the atmosphere of the whole story : " they went out and fled from the tomb : for trembling and astonishment had come upon them : and they said nothing to anyone; for they were afraid."

Now the bewilderment that is so characteristic of Mark's narratives is most apparent in connection with the theme of the suffering of Christ and the glory that lay beyond it. The theme is central both in the sayings of Jesus and in the movement of the narrative.

(1) At Caesarea Philippi Jesus declares that He must die. " The Son of Man must suffer." The teaching is again and again renewed. " The Son of Man shall be delivered unto the chief priests and the scribes; and they shall condemn him to death, and they shall deliver him unto the Gentiles, and they shall mock him and shall spit on him, and shall scourge him, and shall kill him." " Verily the Son of Man came not to be ministered unto but to minister and to give his life a

ransom for many." Inexorably, by a bewildering divine necessity, the story moves from Galilee to Jerusalem, from the scene of Messianic power and blessing to the scene of death. The death is died in utter loneliness. The only recorded word from the Cross is the cry of dereliction. In lonely darkness Jesus dies; and Pilate grants the corpse to Joseph of Arimathaea, who buries it in a tomb. The humiliation of the Servant of the LORD is complete : nothing but the corpse remains, to visit and to care for.

(2) But beyond the humiliation there is the victory predicted. In the predictions use is made, as we saw, of a variety of images. Jesus speaks of the coming of the Kingdom of God with power, of the banquet new with the disciples in the Kingdom of God, of a rising again of the shepherd of the flock, and of the coming of the Son of Man in glory. Asked by Caiaphas in the Sanhedrin whether He is the Christ, Jesus answers :

> "I am; and ye shall see the Son of Man sitting at the right hand of power, and coming with the clouds of heaven." (xiv. 62.)

It seems wrong to infer from these words that Jesus is speaking of a coming in the far distant future. Luke may be interpreting the meaning correctly when he adds the words "from henceforth." Jesus is using imagery drawn from the Book of Daniel : the imagery tells of the triumph and reign of the Son of Man, and that triumph will not be delayed. Just now the Messiah is humiliated, struck and spat upon : He shall be seen reigning and victorious. To this victorious coming, beyond the Cross, Jesus is now directing Caiaphas as He had in the past directed the disciples. His reign will come : and those whom He has made ready will *see*.

With this theme of suffering and glory in his mind the reader of Mark's Gospel passes on to what is now the concluding section.

> "And when the sabbath was past, Mary Magdalene, and Mary the mother of James, and Salome, bought spices that

they might come and anoint him. And very early on the first day of the week, they come to the tomb when the sun was risen. And they were saying among themselves, Who shall roll away the stone from the door of the tomb? and looking up, they see that the stone is rolled back: for it was exceeding great. And entering into the tomb, they saw a young man sitting on the right side, arrayed in a white robe; and they were amazed. And he saith unto them, Be not amazed: ye seek Jesus, the Nazarene, which hath been crucified; he is risen; he is not here: behold the place where they laid him! But go tell his disciples and Peter, He goeth before you into Galilee: there shall ye see him, as he said unto you. And they went out, and fled from the tomb: for trembling and astonishment had come upon them: and they said nothing to any one; for they were afraid " (xvi. 1-8.)

The ending may be lost : but the episode in itself is complete. Mark's Gospel is built up from short sections, each containing a separate story that might be told. Here is a story that proclaims the Resurrection, and links it with the theme of humiliation and glory. How often has Mark told a story containing an approach to Jesus and a Word in answer to those who approach. Here it is only the dead body that the women are approaching. But the word spoken to them turns their thoughts away from the dead body of " Jesus, the Nazarene, which hath been crucified " to the coming in glory. He is not here. The day is come. Go, tell the disciples that they will *see Him*. It is a thought of unspeakable awe. They will *see Him*. The women are silent and afraid.

But silence and fear have their own message. They tell, more than words can, of the overwhelming reality of the Resurrection. " It is clear," says Dr. R. H. Lightfoot, " that the silence, fear, trembling and amazement . . . must have had a great role to play within the early Church."[1] By silence

[1] *Locality and Doctrine*, p. 33. If Dr. Lightfoot does not carry conviction in his contention that Mark ended his Gospel at xvi. 8, he has done the great service of drawing attention to the theological teaching of this section in itself as well as of the other Resurrection narratives.

the women tell us what no words can tell us. The resurrection is not as other events in history. It is in truth the Parousia. It is the coming into the world of the life of the world to come.

Matthew

In Matthew the simplicity of Mark's story disappears in the presence of some new motives drawn from the needs of Christian apologetics. For Matthew, conscious of the continuity of the works of God in Israel and in Christ, shews that the Resurrection has the familiar signs of a *Biblical* miracle. He adds the references to the earthquake, the angel of the Lord descending and rolling away the stone, the soldiers on guard becoming like dead men. But the language is not merely portentous. It does not suffice to explain it by the hackneyed phrase that Matthew "heightens the miraculous." The point is that he uses the miracle-language of the Old Testament, and in doing so he says in effect "it was God who wrought this; the God of Israel, now as of old, came to bring deliverance with mighty hand and outstretched arm."

But the most distinctive part of Matthew's narrative is the concluding episode in Galilee. What Galilee means to Matthew is made clear from an early reference to it in his Gospel.

The land of Zebulon and the land of Naphtali
Toward the sea, beyond Jordan,
Galilee of the Gentiles.
The people which sat in darkness
Saw a great light,
And to them which sat in the region and shadow of death
To them did light spring up. (iv. 15-16. Cf. Isa. ix. 1-2.)

Galilee is a symbol of the borders of the Gentile world. Into this world and into every part of the region and shadow of death will the Gospel of God now be proclaimed. In the story-form of a theophany Matthew describes the appearance of Jesus. It is in Galilee, with the missionary associations of the name. It is upon a mountain, for Jesus is the lawgiver, the Moses of the new people of God. But more still, He is the royal Messiah claiming all authority in heaven and on earth; and in the right of His royal sovereignty He commissions the Church to go into all the world, to teach and to baptize. He will be with them; for the Gospel that began with the revelation of "Immanuel, God with us" ends with the promise "Lo I am with you."

He will be with them "unto the end of the world." Here is a difference of emphasis between Mark and Matthew. Mark views the Resurrection as itself the coming of the end: the Son of Man has returned, the age-to-come is breaking in. Matthew rather looks ahead to the Parousia that still lies in the future when he writes. The mission to the nations must first take place, and then the Lord will come again. This difference of emphasis often confronts the reader of the New Testament, and it cannot be removed or explained away. The tension is inescapable. The day is come: yet the day is still to come. The new world has broken in: yet the history of this world continues. It continues however with the sovereignty of the Messiah, in whom is "all power in heaven and on earth," resting upon it.

Luke

Luke's narratives of the Resurrection diverge from Mark to a greater extent than do Matthew's, both in literary sources and in theological themes. If Mark shews us the Resurrection as the breaking into history of a transcendental act of God, Luke shews rather the place of the Resurrection within that process of history wherein the purpose of God is unfolded.

For whereas Mark describes both the Passion and the message of the Resurrection as it were from near at hand, each event being terrible, staggering and unintelligible, Luke tells the story as it were from a point further away, whence the events can be seen in their intelligible place in the divine scheme of history. All was at first mysterious; but now, Luke seems to say, all possesses a plan that we can know and understand. The plan belongs to God, and it is unfolded in the whole series of acts in the divine drama: the preparation, the birth, the childhood, the baptism, the ministry, the Passion, the Resurrection, the promise of the Father, the journey of the Gospel to all the world. Ought not men to realize how inevitable each step in the plan has been?

> "Beloved it not the Christ to suffer these things, and to enter into his glory?" (xxiv. 26.)
> "Thus it is written, that the Christ should suffer and rise again from the dead the third day : and that repentance and remission of sins should be preached in his name unto all nations beginning from Jerusalem." (xxiv. 46-47.)

What was at the first impact miraculous and unintelligible has become, without ceasing to be miraculous, truly "natural" and intelligible. Hence Luke suggests in his narratives that the Resurrection ought to have been expected, known and understood.

> "Why seek ye the living among the dead?" (xxiv. 5.)
> "Remember how he spake unto you. . . ." (xxiv. 6.)
> "O foolish men, and slow of heart to believe in all that the prophets have spoken!" (xxiv. 25.)

For Luke history and theology are one; and, if he shews us less than does Mark of the Resurrection as a supra-historical coming of the Day of the LORD, he draws out instead the important truth that in the Resurrection one epoch of history, human and divine, reaches its climax and another epoch has its beginning. He teaches the truths upon which Westcott was to lay great emphasis : "what was before miraculous is now natural." "The Resurrection is the central point of history, primarily of religious history, and then of civil history of which that is the soul" (*Gospel of the Resurrection*, p. 6).

If therefore Mark's rugged story leaves the reader awe-struck, Luke's sensitive and human narrative brings the Resurrection home to mind and heart and conscience. He leads his readers to reflect upon its relation to God, to Christ, to history, to themselves. He draws together Cross and Resurrection, with a hint of the Johannine Cross-glory theme.

Above all, he shews that the Resurrection does not touch the world at a tangent. It is attested by bodily evidences: " handle me and see, for a spirit hath not flesh and bones as ye see me having." It belongs to the historical order. It reaches down to the thought and feeling of men and women; it kindles their understanding, and it evokes their worship.

For it is in *worship* that Luke's Gospel ends, as it begins. In the beginning Zacharias is in the temple worshipping in the order of his priestly course. At the conclusion, the disciples are in the temple worshipping and blessing God. The scene is the same: but the meaning of worship has been transformed by the Resurrection.

(1) It was in the breaking of the bread that the self-revelation of Jesus at Emmaus took place. Till then, the two disciples had not recognized Him. Was this meal the Eucharist? The phrase used is a regular term for the Eucharist (cf. Acts xx. 7), and the minds of Luke's Christian readers would turn inevitably to what has been called " the sacred feast wherein Christ is received, the memory of the Passion is renewed, the mind is filled with grace, and a pledge of glory to come is given unto us." If we cannot be sure of the precise character of the meal and action at Emmaus we can notice this significant parallelism: Jesus in the blessing and breaking of the bread in the Upper Room unfolded the meaning of His Passion, Jesus in the blessing and breaking of the bread at Emmaus unfolded to two disciples the fact of his Resurrection. For the early Christians the breaking of the bread was a central link both with the Passion and the Resurrection; and in the Eucharistic rite the people of Christ still shew forth His death and feed upon His life, and Calvary and Easter are perpetuated in the life of the Church.

(2) Finally, Jesus leads the Apostles from Jerusalem to a place over against Bethany; and He lifts up His hands and blesses them and is parted from them. Their response to this last visible act is *to worship Jesus* and, returning to Jerusalem, *to bless God*. Henceforth the worship of Jesus and the praise of God are inseparably blended. Without any weakening of the monotheism of their fathers the disciples in Jerusalem continued to worship Jesus, risen and exalted at the right

hand of God. They expressed their devotion by calling Him Lord, and by applying to Him the imagery of "the right hand of God" from Psalm cx. The earliest known credal formula is "Jesus is Lord." *Lex orandi lex credendi.* Within the primitive worship of Jesus by the disciples in Jerusalem the whole rich development of the doctrine of His Person in the Apostolic Age is implicitly contained. For to worship Jesus is to affirm that all that is true of God is true of Him.

John

In the Fourth Gospel the narratives of the Resurrection, to a greater degree than the narratives in the other Gospels, reflect the special themes of the evangelist.

The central theme of the Fourth Gospel, as we saw earlier, is Life. The words and works of the Christ are a manifestation of Life, and they extend to the whole range of human needs, spiritual and bodily alike. The healing of the sick and impotent, the feeding of the hungry, the giving of sight to the blind, the raising of Lazarus from death, are all signs of the life-giving mission of the Son of God. The Life is the life of the age to come, the "aeonian" life, realized already in the present age. It is received by believing on Christ and by feeding on Him. He is Himself the Life. To possess Life is to know the Father and the Son.

Thus is Life manifested. But, as with the Kingdom of God in the Synoptic narrative, so with the Life in John's narrative, the full manifestation must await the Passion. The haunting words "not yet" recur in the story. "Mine hour is not yet come." "My time is not yet at hand." "Jesus was not yet glorified." For the Life is in its essence a Life that is given, laid-down, surrendered; and its character is wrought out and bestowed by the historical Death and Resurrection of Jesus.

"Therefore doth the Father love me, because I lay down my life, that I may take it again. No one taketh it away from me, but I lay it down of myself. I have power to lay it down and I have power to take it again. This commandment received I from the Father." (x. 17-18.)

The story therefore moves towards the death in Jerusalem. The death and resurrection of Lazarus is a preliminary parable of the great events. The corn of wheat must fall to the earth and die (xii. 24). The "hour" comes. Jesus dies on the Cross, while the passover lambs are being slain for sacrifice.

The Death and the Resurrection, wherein the Gospel of Life is wrought out, are described by John in close relation one to another. As we saw, the note of victory resounds through the story of the Passion. Even in death there is life-giving-power, as is symbolized by the flowing of blood and water from the side of Jesus pierced by the spear of the soldier. Blood means life: water means cleansing. Both have been the themes of the words and works of Jesus throughout the Gospel; and both are now released freely for mankind through the Passion. But if there is Life present in Death, there is also the note of Death still to be heard in the midst of Life. For the marks of Calvary remain; and it is with wounded hands and side that the risen Jesus gives His peace to the disciples.

Here is Life eternal—revealed, wrought out, bestowed. The " not yet " that has cast its shadow across the story is no more. For " that hour " came on Calvary (xix. 27), and " that day " came at Easter (xx. 19). And now by the gift of the Paraclete the fruits of life are made available for men.

It is with these theological themes in mind that John writes his narratives of the Resurrection. He views the events of Easter as the climax of these themes and as the fulfilment of the promises made at the Supper. But while he writes as an interpreting theologian he is at pains to shew that here as elsewhere the theology is rooted in history. Nor is his history far removed from that of the Synoptists. Whether he had the narratives of the Synoptists before him (as many modern scholars believe) or whether he used independent traditions (as Mr. Gardner-Smith has powerfully argued), his material is in many ways *akin* to that used by the earlier evangelists. Akin to *Mark's* story of the women at the tomb is John's story of Mary Magdalene at the tomb. Akin to *Matthew's* closing scene in Galilee is John's deliberate use of a Galilean tradition with a missionary motive; for the episode of the fishing on the lake seems full of the symbolism of the Church's mission to catch fish on the seas of the heathen world. Akin to *Luke* is John's record of the appearance of Jesus to the eleven in Jerusalem. It is in essence the same history that forms John's basis. But he sees the history in the fuller light of the Church's knowledge of Him who is the Way, the Truth, the Life.

It is when John's narratives are contrasted with Luke's that his view of the relation between theology and history becomes most apparent.

Like Luke, John insists upon the historical character of the Resurrection and upon the evidence of touch and sight. (i.) Luke had alluded to a visit of some disciples to the tomb to verify the story told by the women. According to some MSS. he also recorded explicitly a visit of Peter who ran to the tomb, saw the linen clothes by themselves, and departed wondering. John describes this event more fully. It was, he says, the beloved disciple who, with Peter, ran to the tomb. The beloved disciple reached the tomb first, stooped and looked in, but did not enter. Peter then arrived, entered and saw. But it was the beloved disciple who both saw and believed, convinced by the sight of the linen lying deprived of its use and yet in perfect order. The evidence of sight was convincing. (ii.) So too was the evidence of sight convincing when Jesus on the evening of Easter day shewed the disciples His hands and His side (cf. Luke xxiv. 39, " his hands and his feet ") and they rejoiced to see Him (cf. Luke xxiv. 41). (iii.) So too was the evidence of sight convincing in the case of Thomas. Here Jesus offered the use of the further evidence of touch. Incredulous, Thomas had said that he would never believe until he had touched the wounds of Jesus. Jesus invited him to have the evidence which he sought. But it was not needed : without touching, Thomas saw and believed. None the less, those who have not seen and yet have believed are blessed.

For in contrast to Luke's emphasis upon evidence and history is John's insistence that evidence and history, though they matter supremely, cannot of themselves be intelligible or reveal God. The action of the Holy Spirit is needed to enable men to perceive the meaning of history. This is a recurring theme of the Fourth Gospel. Men must look through and beyond the facts of history to the Truth which history discloses; and they cannot do this without the aid of the Spirit. Flesh is of inescapable importance: the Word was made flesh: he who would know God must face the deeds of Jesus in the flesh: he must eat the flesh of the Son of Man and drink His blood. But of itself the flesh profiteth nothing; it is the spirit that quickeneth.

Such being his teaching, when John reaches the narratives of the Resurrection he is at one with Luke in emphasizing the importance of the visible and tangible evidences. But he is also insistent, as Luke is not, on turning the mind of the reader to the invisible realities which give the events their meaning.

Among these invisible realities are *the Father* and *the Spirit*. He who would understand the Resurrection must learn that it is the road whereby Jesus goes to the Father; and that only through the new creation wrought by the Spirit can men know the risen Christ. "Touch me not, for I am not yet ascended to the Father." "Jesus breathed on them and said, Receive ye the Holy Spirit."

The Father

Throughout His early life Jesus is going to the Father. Though He is one with the Father from all eternity He has been made one with mankind, and He journeys to the Father along the road of human life and death. If sometimes the word used is ἀναβάινω to "go up" or "ascend," more often it is simply ὑπάγω or πορεύομαι the ordinary words for a journey. "Yet a little while I am with you, and I go unto him that sent me" (vii. 33). The unbelieving Jews cannot follow Him upon the journey. To them the way is self-barred: "Ye shall seek me, and shall not find me; and where I am, ye cannot come" (vii. 34). But the disciples will be enabled, in the end, to follow Him: "where I am, there shall also my servant be" (xii. 26). "I go . . . that where I am, there ye may be also" (xiv. 3). "Father . . . I will that, where I am, they also may be with me, that they may behold my glory" (xvii. 24). But they cannot follow Him now: as yet, He must go alone upon a solitary journey, separated from them as He leaves the world.

The departure of Jesus throws the disciples into desolation. But in His discourse at the Supper He tells them of its necessity, and of its coming fruits. It is expedient. It will enable the coming of an entirely new order in which they will share. For He will come again to them (xiv. 3). Both He and His Father will make their abode with those who love Him and keep His words (xiv. 23). They will be enabled to do works greater than those which He has done (xiv. 12). The Paraclete will help them to recollect and to understand what He has said (xiv. 26), and He will take of the things of Jesus and declare them to the disciples (xvi. 14). They will see Jesus (xvi. 16). Their joy will overflow (xvi. 22). Their access to the Father will be such that there need be no limit to the boldness of their petitions (xvi. 23). No longer will Jesus speak to them in riddles, He will tell them plainly of the Father (xvi. 25). All this will be the fruit of His lonely journey to the Father. Let there be no clinging to Jesus. He has shared hitherto in the mode of their earthly existence : He goes away that through tribulation He may lead them to share in His new life, to the Father's glory. These things will happen " in *that day* " (xvi. 26).

" Arise let us go hence." Jesus goes out to tread the last stages of the road to the Father. The Passion and the Resurrection were that road : but they did not of themselves complete it. Easter morning dawned; Mary saw Jesus; and yet there was still a further step to be trod. For when Mary wished to cling to Him by the tomb He said to her,

" Touch me not; for I am not yet ascended unto the Father."

She must not cling to Him, desiring His presence after the manner of the former days when He shared in this earth's ways of touch. The old ways are about to give place to new. Jesus is on His way up to the Father; and, when the journey is perfected, then there will be touch between Him and those who are His, after a new manner. Therefore He says : Do not touch me now, but

> " go to my brethren, and say to them, I am going up unto my Father and your Father, my God and your God."

The ascent will be accomplished forthwith. There need be no more delay. The "not yet" will pass away. "That day," dawning already, will be realized. The Father, to whom Jesus is going, is the Father of the disciples also. Yet there is a difference : He says not "our Father," but "my Father and your Father": His sonship is from all eternity, theirs is bestowed and derived from His.

The Holy Spirit

The journey to the Father was completed on Easter Day. Then followed on "that day" at evening the gift of Holy Spirit to the disciples; and the gift has been made possible by the completion of the journey. Far back in the story John has said that the gift of Holy Spirit is made possible only by the Passion and Exaltation of Jesus (vii. 39). For Holy Spirit is given so as to reproduce in the disciples "the things of Jesus," namely the Life-through-death which is the essence of His life. "When therefore it was evening on that day, the first day of the week . . . Jesus came and stood in the midst." He had spoken at the supper of "that day," and now that day is come. He speaks Peace unto them. They are filled with joy. He shews unto them His hands and His side.

> " Jesus therefore said to them again, Peace be unto you : as the Father hath sent me, even so send I you. And when he had said this, he breathed on them, and saith unto them, Receive ye the Holy Ghost : whose soever sins ye forgive, they are forgiven unto them; whose soever sins ye retain, they are retained." (xx. 21-23.)

Here is an act of *new creation*. The breath of Jesus recalls

" The LORD God formed man out of the dust of the ground and breathed into his nostrils the breath of life, and man became a living soul" (Gen. ii. 7). Paul says: "The last Adam became a life-giving spirit" (1 Cor. xv. 45). There have perhaps been hints of a new creation already in John's narrative: the voice of the Lord in the garden. Here too, consequent upon the new creation, is the *Apostolic mission.* It is akin to the mission of Jesus from the Father, for "as Thou didst send me into the world, even so sent I them into the world" (xvii. 18). The end of the mission is the release of mankind from sin, that through the disciples the mercy and judgment wrought by the Passion and the Resurrection may be brought to bear upon human lives. Thus the disciples will forgive sins and retain them. This commission is given to the whole Church. It includes the specific ministry of absolution, it includes (perhaps more directly) the baptism with water and the Spirit. It comprises the entire office of the Church to bring to mankind the cleansing made possible by the Cross.

It is clear that John wishes his readers to understand that the Ascension took place on Easter Day. This is in contrast with the account by Luke, where the Ascension is described (Acts i. 9) as happening at the close of the series of appearances during forty days. The contradiction seems puzzling. The present writer would make this suggestion. Perhaps Luke and John have different happenings in mind. John is, in xx. 17, alluding to (for he could never describe) the journey of Jesus to the Father's glory, a going to the Father which though it involves historical events is essentially beyond history. Luke is describing in a concrete picture an event whereby Jesus gave to the disciples a visible assurance that the appearances were ended. There seems no inconsistency between the truth which John is teaching and the event which Luke is recording.

It is harder to understand the "contradiction" between the story of the gift of the Spirit on Easter Day as John records it and the story of Pentecost as Luke records it. But here the possibility that there was a twofold gift need not be excluded. The Holy Spirit overshadowed the manhood of Jesus both at His conception and at His baptism. Subsequently the Holy Spirit endows the people of Christ both in baptism and in the laying-on-of-hands. Similarly a twofold action may have occurred in the original redemptive events : on Easter Day, a bestowal of the breath of the new life; at Pentecost, an outpouring for the execution of those tasks which the new life involved.

John is eager to shew that when once the day is come, then fulfilment and realization follow quickly. It is clear from the New Testament as a whole that the Resurrection implies the breaking-into-history of the age-to-come. But as we have seen, the evangelists treat the story of the Resurrection in rather different ways in relation to this eschatological theme. *Mark* seems to tell of the Resurrection as the Parousia : the day of the Son of Man. *Matthew* thinks rather of the world-wide task that still awaits the Church before the Parousia, which is still in the future. *Luke* brings the Resurrection more closely to the continuous movement of history of which Jesus Christ is the Lord. *John,* like Mark, dwells upon the realization of the end. To a greater extent than any other writer he shews that eternal life is come : Easter is the day of fulfilment : the things predicted at the Supper are here.

But, for John, there is also a consummation yet to come. Eternal life is here; the victory has been won. But still the disciples must toil all night upon the lake; and one will be girded and carried whither he would not to a martyr's death, and another may tarry until the Lord shall come. But, whether they die or whether they tarry, what is it? For to those who believe in the Resurrection of Christ it is always the " last hour."

CHAPTER VII

The Resurrection and the Church

I

A BOOK whose subject is the Resurrection of Christ inevitably includes a treatment of the Church. We cannot separate "Christ the firstfruits" and "they that are Christ's," or (as we might well translate) "they that belong to the Messiah" (1 Cor. xv. 23). The word "Christ" itself implies the community over which the Messiah reigns. Nowhere has the relation of Church and Christ been better summed up than in the words of Emile Mersch in his book *Le Corps Mystique du Christ*: "Les Evangiles n'en parlent pas directement; directement ils ne parlent que de Jésus. Mais précisément le Jésus dont ils parlent n'est pas un Jésus tout limité et tout fermé an lui-même." (p. 25.)

Some modern writers are puzzled by what appears to them to be a scarcity of teaching given by Jesus Christ concerning the Church, and they conclude that the Church therefore cannot be one of the important elements in Christianity. The same method of argument would lead to the conclusion that the Holy Spirit or the Resurrection itself has an unimportant place in Christianity; for how few are the sayings of Jesus, in the first three Gospels, concerning either of these themes! But a wrong approach is apparent here. If Jesus came to teach a Gospel, He came also to *be*, in His whole life and death and Resurrection and Pentecost, a Gospel: some of the most significant parts of His mission lie beyond His own words as Rabbi or teacher. So with the Church: Jesus did not found a Church by giving a set of instructions as if it were a kind of society for the followers of a teacher. The Church existed already; it was Israel. Jesus summed up the mission of Israel in His own person as Son and Servant. He gathered a remnant around Him, and became Himself the centre and the stem of a new Israel constituted by His Resurrection from death. It is in *Him,* and especially in His Resurrection, that the basis of the Church appears. In this, as in all else, Christianity is an Easter Faith.

None the less, the most distinct seeds of the Church can be noted in the teaching of Jesus, deliberately and patiently sown. The Messiah addressed His message to Israel: summoning Israel to repent. But as the nation as a whole was unresponsive He gathered around Him a remnant as the nucleus of an Israel to be. Gladly would He have gathered all Jerusalem's children as a hen gathers her brood under her wings (Matt. xxiii. 37), but they would not. He gathers instead the "little flock" of the disciples (Luke xii. 32). In every startum of the literary sources of the Gospels we find sayings of Jesus about this theme. He appoints twelve "that they might be with him, and that he might send them forth" (Mark iii. 14). That they are twelve in number is specially significant, for Jesus is reconstituting the Israel of God symbolized by the twelve tribes (cf. Matt. xix. 18=Luke xxii. 30). To the twelve Jesus declares on the night before the Passion the new covenant in His blood (Mark xiv. 24); and a covenant implies a People of God with whom it is made. Once more an Israel is to be set free by a mighty act of God, to serve Him and to be His people.

But the realization of all this lies in the future. The little flock was scattered when the blow fell upon its shepherd; they forsook Him and fled. He died alone. But He died as Israel's true representative, Himself the remnant of Israel, the true vine. And He was raised from death to be the head of a new Israel formed from those of every race and nation, who receive His gift of forgiveness and by faith and baptism make His death their own and become united to His risen life. The confession of the early Christians is "Jesus is Lord," a confession springing from the belief that God raised Him from death and exalted Him. They make this confession as members of His ecclesia, and they are able to do so only by the aid of the Spirit of the risen Jesus (1 Cor. xii. 3, Rom. x. 8-9). They are baptized into His death and are made sharers in His Resurrection. Such is the origin and the meaning of the Church.

In two important sayings recorded in the Gospels the connection between the Church and the Resurrection is apparent.

(1) The first is the saying before the Passion about the smiting of the shepherd and the scattering of the sheep. The imagery of the shepherd in the New Testament is used more than once with the Resurrection in mind.

> ". . . it is written, I will smite the shepherd, and the sheep shall be scattered abroad. Howbeit, after I am raised up I will go before you into Galilee." (Mark xiv. 27-28.)

We may compare the shepherd-sayings in the Fourth Gospel, where too the shepherd dies for the flock and rises from death.

> "And other sheep I have, which are not of this fold; them also I must bring, and they shall hear my voice: and they shall become one flock, one shepherd. Therefore doth my Father love me, because I lay down my life, that I may take it again." (John x. 16-17.)

Of old God had "brought his people up out of the sea with the shepherd of his flock" (Is. lxii. 11). Now God raised the shepherd from death to unite the flock and to draw together many sheep. The theme recurs in the Epistle to the Hebrews:

> "Now the God of peace, who brought again from the dead the great shepherd of the sheep with the blood of the eternal covenant, even our Lord Jesus, make you perfect in every good thing to do his will, working in us that which is well-pleasing in his sight." (Heb. xiii. 20-21.)

Without the Resurrection the flock is scattered and perishing.

(2) The second saying, which specially draws out the truth about the Church and the Resurrection and indeed sums it up, is at the close of the narrative of the cleansing of the temple in the Fourth Gospel.

> "The Jews therefore answered and said unto him, What

sign shewest thou unto us, seeing that thou doest these things? Jesus answered and said unto them, Destroy this temple, and in three days I will raise it up. The Jews therefore said, Forty and six years was this temple in building and wilt thou raise it up in three days? But he spake of the temple of his body. When therefore he was raised from the dead, his disciples remembered that he spake this : and they believed the scripture, and the word which Jesus had said." (John ii. 18-22.)

The theme is not only Johannine. It is clear from earlier documents that Jesus was accused of threatening to destroy the temple made with hands and to replace it in three days by a temple made without hands (Mark xiv. 58, xv. 29). It is also recorded that He said that a rejected stone would become the head of the corner in a new building (Mark xii. 10). Here in the Fourth Gospel the story of the cleansing of the temple and the words which follow sum up the ending of the old order and the coming of the new. As Hoskyns pointed out, the word λύω is used both of the destruction of a building and the dissolution of human life : here it indicates both the death of the body of Jesus and the destruction of the system which centred in the temple and its worship. In its place there will be raised up " the temple of his body " : a temple in which Christ's people will be the stones, a body in which Christ's people will be the members. Judaism will be replaced by the risen Christ and the Christians united to Him. They will be both the temple of God (cf. 1 Cor. iii. 16-17, Eph. ii. 21, 1 Peter ii. 5) and the body of Christ (cf. 1 Cor. xii. 27, Eph. i. 22-23). These great Apostolic doctrines have their roots in the ministry of Jesus. Without the Church His mission is incomplete, but without the Resurrection the Church is an idle name.

II

It is clear from the Gospels that our Lord is, in Mersch's words, "pas un Jésus tout limité et tout fermé en lui-même"; and the same is clear from the Epistles. The mem-

bers of the new Church are so closely united to the risen
Christ that His life is described by Paul as including theirs.

"For the love of Christ constraineth us; because we thus
judge that one died for all, therefore all died; and he died
for all, that they which live should no longer live unto
themselves, but unto him who for their sakes died and
rose again. Wherefore we henceforth know no man after
the flesh: even though we have known Christ after the
flesh, yet now we know him so no more." (2 Cor. v.
14-16.)

Dying to their own self-centredness, the Christians enter a new
life wherein the centre is not themselves but the risen Christ.
No longer do they think of Christ only in terms of His
existence in history as an isolated figure: for they think of
Him as risen and contemporary and embracing His people
as a very part of His own life. It is this that lies behind the
description of the Christians as "the Body of Christ."

It is uncertain how the phrase "the Body of Christ" came
into existence as a description of the Church. One suggestion
is that its origin is derived from the imagery of the Eucharist
wherein the Christians are one body by partaking of the body
of Christ (cf. Rawlinson in *Mysterium Christi*, pp. 225 ff.).
Another suggestion is that the phrase is derived from contemporary Stoic uses of the word *soma* (cf. W. L. Knox, *S.
Paul and the Church of the Gentiles*, pp. 160 ff.). But it is
clear that whatever the origin of the verbal form may be, the
truth that it expresses is created by the Resurrection of Christ
and the impact of the Resurrection upon the first Christians.
The emphasis in the phrase "Body of Christ" is upon the
word *of Christ*. The Christians are *His* Body, the sphere of
the action of *His* risen life.

From the day of his conversion Paul is made aware of a true
solidarity between the risen Christ and the disciples. "Saul,
Saul, why persecutest thou *me*?" He knows that Christ is one
with His persecuted followers and suffers with them. Hence it
is to no solitary Christ that Paul is converted, but to a Christ
whose disciples are indeed His "body." Some incidental

references in the Epistles shew the link between the risen
Christ and the Christians.

"The body is not for fornication, but for the Lord; and
the Lord for the body: and God both raised the Lord, and
will raise up us through his power. Know ye not that
your bodies are members of Christ?" (1 Cor. vi. 13-15.)

Here Paul is speaking of the human bodies of Christian
people, united to the risen Lord so as to be indeed *His*
members. Compare and contrast these words:

"Wherefore, my brethren, ye also were made dead to the
law, through the body of Christ: that ye should be joined
to another, even to him that was raised from the dead, that
we might bring forth fruit unto God." (Rom. vii. 4.)

Here the death of the body of Christ upon the Cross is the
means whereby the Christians have been "joined" to Christ
raised from death.

These passages are but casual references. For this very
reason they have great significance, for they disclose a truth
which is in the Apostle's mind concerning the Resurrection
and the Church. The truth is drawn out fully in some other
expository passages. There is first the comparison between
Christ and the Christians and *a* body:

"For as the body is one, and hath many members, and
all the members of the body being many are one body; so
also in Christ." (1 Cor. xii. 12.)

Then there is the direct *description* of the Christians as *His*
Body:

"now ye are the body of Christ, and severally members
thereof." (1 Cor. xii. 27.)

Finally there is the sublime summary in the Epistle to the
Ephesians. Here the description of the exaltation of Christ in

the heavenly places, supreme over all, is followed by the daring assertion that He is incomplete without the Church which is both His Body and His fulness. Paul prays that God may lead the Christians to a realization of the exceeding greatness of His power, wrought in Christ,

> " when he raised him from the dead, and made him to sit at his right hand in the heavenly places . . . and he put all things in subjection under his feet, and gave him to be head over all things to the church which is his body, the fulness of him that filleth all in all." (Eph. i. 20-23.)

The exalted Christ is incomplete without the Church. It is through the Church that He lives and works. The essence of the Church is not the members who belong to it but the Christ from whom its life is derived. It is He, and not they, that provides the Church's foundation.

But the foundation of the Church upon the Resurrection implies for it a constant relation to the Passion also. It is by baptism into the death of Christ that we are made His members, and it is by a continually renewed relation to His death that our membership is sustained.

The New Testament shews how the Christian life thus began and thus continued. The convert reaches out by faith from himself to Christ who died for him, renouncing the life-unto-self. He plunges beneath the waters of baptism as one who dies, and he emerges into a new life in Christ who rose again. " Are ye ignorant, that all we who were baptized into Christ Jesus were baptized into His death?" (Rom. vi. 3). But the convert's relation to the Cross does not cease there. The living Christ, to whom he now belongs, is still Christ the crucified one; and the Christian advances in " the fellowship of his sufferings, being conformed unto his death " (Phil. iii. 10). If once for all he has " died with Christ " (Col. iii. 3) he is not exempt from the subsequent command " mortify therefore your members which are upon the earth " (Col. iii. 5). He is ever near to the Cross in his own conflict with sin; in his bearing of sorrow, pain and humiliation when they come to him; in his bearing of the pains of others; in his increasing knowledge of what Calvary meant and means. But in all this he is discovering that the risen life of Jesus belongs to him, and with it great rejoicing. Awhile perhaps it may be that the Cross is more apparent to him, and the risen life may seem to be hidden. But one day the secret that is already present will be made manifest, and in the Resurrection that awaits him after death he will see the risen Christ in whose life, though hidden, he has already shared.

Cross and Resurrection are the ground of the Church's origin, the secret of the Church's contemporary being, the goal of the Church's final self-realization on behalf of the human race. The Word and the Sacraments in the midst of the Church make known to its members continually what is their origin, their secret and their goal. For the *Word* is the Word of the Cross, whereby the Church is made, renewed and judged. The *Eucharist* is the proclaiming of the Lord's death until His coming again; the setting forth before God and man of the whole drama of His life, death, Resurrection and Parousia; and the feeding of His people with His broken body and outpoured blood. The Eucharist looks back to the events of the Gospel; it realizes those events in the present hour; it anticipates the final consummation : " the Body of our Lord Jesus Christ which was given for thee preserve thy body and soul unto everlasting life."

III

The treasure is in earthen vessels; and herein lies the paradox of the Church as it is known in history. On the one hand it contains a divine life and is constituted by that divine life; on the other hand its members are sinful and entangled in the world. The paradox is not new. The Church was never otherwise. The rather romantic tendency of the writer of Acts does not prevent him from describing the deceit of Ananias and Sapphira, and the bickering of the widows about the dole. Paul's realism about the moral failures of the Christians of Corinth does not prevent him from asserting that Christ is in them, wisdom and righteousness and sanctification, and that they are indeed His Body. At once the Church contains the hidden life of Christ and a host of sinful contradictions. "Who is blind, but my servant?"

This paradox provides the historian of the Church with his biggest problems and the good man who studies the contemporary Church in any age with his biggest perplexity. Conscious of the hindrance to Christianity which the paradox affords, Christians have often been led to conclude that the Church cannot after all be an important element in essential Christianity and that real Christianity can be presented without much reference to it. This conclusion is in its turn difficult because it violates the evidence of the New Testament that there is a very close connection between the Gospel and the Church, evidence which recent critical study has tended to enhance. But there have been other ways of escape; and Christians have sought to escape from the paradox of the Church by violent and lopsided doctrines.

(1) One attempted solution has been to regard the true Church as the society of the morally pure and perfect. "Out with the weak and out with those who lapsed under persecution. Out with the harlots and the fornicators. Out with those who fail to reach a certain measurable standard of moral obedience!" This solution has been attempted by many Puritan movements both in early and later centuries. It does violence to the true meaning of the Church. For the holiness of the Church is the holiness of the Spirit whereby the members are made holy. To use visible standards of morality as a test of membership is to transfer the merit and glory from Christ to the members themselves, and to set forth the Church as a society of the moral rather than a family of the redeemed. By this procedure fornication may be expelled, but pride and self-righteousness may eat their way within.

(2) Another solution has been to equate the sovereignty of God and the sovereignty of the visible Church upon earth, so as to identify the visible Church with the Kingdom of God itself. This solution has been attended by disastrous results. It violates the distinction apparent in the New Testament between the Kingdom and the Church. For the Kingdom means primarily not the realm but the reign or sovereignty of God: and of this reign, which comes by the way of the

Cross, the Church is the servant and the herald. The Kingdom is brought to men through the Church and is found within it: but it always transcends the Church. Attempts to solve the problem of the Church by thus exaggerating its meaning have led to equally violent and one-sided reactions.

(3) Yet another solution is familiar, born of reaction against the last. This is to view the true Church as properly invisible and ideal, laid up in heaven, and to regard the empirical Church upon earth as being not really the true Church. This solution includes the belief that a right understanding of the spiritual and heavenly nature of the Church will lead to an indifference to its visible order and its sacramental continuity. This solution likewise contradicts the nature of New Testament Christianity. For the visible Body with its God-given sacraments and its God-given ministry does matter. The Church belongs to history as well as to heaven, to flesh as well as to spirit. It bears witness to the historical Incarnation of God. It is "sent" historically by Jesus Christ even as He was "sent" by the Father. It links men with the Cross and the Resurrection as historical events. Men truly know the Church of heaven if they are humble enough to bear the pains and paradoxes of the visible Church upon earth.

Each of these attempts to make the Church less paradoxical involves a false short-cut and a denial of truth. For the New Testament will not ease the paradox for us: it allows us to overlook neither the truth that the Church is the Body of Christ nor the existence of Christians who crucify the Son of God afresh and put him to a perpetual shame. But the New Testament suggests that the way is to accept the paradox, not with complaisance nor with a sense of grievance but with the light of the Cross and Resurrection upon it. The man who knows, from the Cross, his own need is not ashamed to put himself beside the other members of the Church whose need is like his own; and to discover amid the contradictions of the Church's members the risen life of Christ which is the divine answer to his needs as to theirs.

IV

It is however not only in the New Testament that the Biblical meaning of the Church is disclosed. For just as the Resurrection sent the Apostles back to the Old Testament in their understanding of Jesus Christ, so it sends us back to the Old Testament to find there some permanent truths about the Church in its relation to God and to the world. As Augustine said, "obscurius dixerunt prophetae de Christo quam de Ecclesia" (*in Psa.* xxx.).

The Church of Israel was called by God not to glorify itself but to make Him known to the nations. It possessed an imperishability, not on account of any merits of its members but on account of the faithfulness of God who wills to use Israel for the redemption of mankind. When Israel fails, the judgment of God falls and punishment follows : yet there is a remnant whom God uses as the stump from which a new and better tree may grow. God does not find the Israelites of any particular generation to be indispensable : He is not pledged to them, if they are unfaithful to Him; He can sweep them aside, and from the stones of a heathen world He can raise up new ones who will serve Him better. But Israel continues imperishable, even if its true mission be represented by a very small number or by the lonely Christ, who bears the destiny of Israel to Calvary and to the grave.

For the God of Israel is the God who judges and raises up. His people come to learn of Him and to make Him known not by the even tenor of a steady spiritual growth, but through crises of judgment and resurrection. Great deliverances and times of spiritual prosperity are followed by the disasters born of pride and complacency : humiliation follows, and in the day of humiliation God raises up His servants and prophets. What is true of the old Israel is true also of the new. Centuries of achievement lead on to stagnation and self-sufficiency, and the God who raised up Moses, Amos, Jeremiah, Ezra raises up Benedict, Francis, Wesley, Keble. The Church is judged when it gives the glory to itself : it is renewed only by accepting the judgment and by being raised again to seek the glory of God in the service of mankind.

But if the comparison between the old Israel and the new is important, it is no less important to notice where the contrast lies. It lies most chiefly in the fact that whereas the old Israel was sustained by repeated actions of God in raising her up, the new Israel has behind it and within it the one, final, decisive Passion and Resurrection of Christ. Her mission is to make His Passion and Resurrection known, so that mankind may learn in the midst of every historical crisis both the judgment and the mercy which the Passion and Resurrection bring. And she fulfils her mission only by being brought herself again and again beneath that judgment and mercy which she teaches to mankind. " Rejoice not against me, O mine enemy : when I fall, I shall arise; when I sit in darkness, the Lord shall be a light unto me. I will bear the indignation of the Lord, because I have sinned against him; until he plead my cause, and execute judgment for me : he will bring me forth to the light, and I shall behold his righteousness " (Micah vii. 8-9).

CHAPTER VIII

The Resurrection of the Dead

THE belief in " the Resurrection of the Body " has been a stumbling-block both in the ancient and in the modern world. In the beginning, no doctrine could have been better chosen for exciting ridicule in Athens and disbelief in Corinth. In these latter days, it has been almost an axiom of liberal theology that the clause needs either removing or else interpreting as equivalent to the immortality of the soul. Yet to have succumbed to the objectors, either in the old world or the new, would have been a disaster. It would have blunted the cutting-edge of the Gospel and removed a doctrine which sums up the genius of Christianity in its belief about man and the world. To-day, with the recovery of a truly Biblical perspective and with the abandonment of a rigid antithesis between spirit and matter, the wheel has turned; and it does not seem strange or surprising to read this confession made by Dr. Niebuhr :

" These closing words of the Apostolic creed, in which the Christian hope of the fulfilment of life is expressed, were, as I remember it, an offence and a stumbling-block to young theologians at the time when my generation graduated from the theological seminaries. Those of us who were expected to express our Christian faith in terms of the Apostolic Creed at the occasion of our ordination had long and searching discussions on the problem presented by the Creed, particularly by this last phrase. We were not certain that we could honestly express our faith in such a formula. If we were finally prevailed upon to do so, it was usually with a patronising air towards the Christian past, with which we desired to express a sense of unity even if the price was the suppression of our moral and theological scruples over its rendering of the Christian faith.

The twenty years which divide that time from this have brought great changes in theological thought, though I am not certain that many of my contemporaries are not still of the same mind in which they were then. Yet some of us have been persuaded to take the stone which we then rejected and to make it the head of the corner. In other words there is no part of the Apostolic Creed which, in our present opinion, expresses the whole genius of the Christian faith more neatly than just that despised phrase, ' I believe in the Resurrection of the body.' " (*Beyond Tragedy*, pp. 289-290.)

I

While traditional Christianity insists upon distinguishing the revealed doctrine of Resurrection from a philosophical belief in the immortality of the soul, it regards the latter not as untrue and irrelevant so much as incomplete, distressingly dull and missing the gift of the Gospel. There are grounds, both philosophical and psychological and religious, for believing that the soul survives death; though the life of a soul without the body is a conception which it is difficult to imagine. It is *incomplete*; because the self is far more than the soul, and the self without bodily expression can hardly be the complete self. It is *dull*; because it implies the prolongation of man's finite existence for everlasting years. In contrast both with the incompleteness and the dullness of the immortality of the soul Christianity teaches a future state (not as of right but as of God's gift) wherein the soul is not unclothed but clothed upon by a bodily expression, and wherein the finite human life is raised so as to share, without losing its finiteness, in the infinite life of Christ Himself.

The Christian Gospel was not first addressed to people who had *no* belief in a future state. Greeks were familiar with a philosophical doctrine of immortality. Jews believed in the resurrection of the body. Sometimes this was thought of as a resuscitation of human relics and a reconstruction of human existence after the fashion of the present life. Sometimes it was thought of as a transformation of dead bodies into an utterly new state of glory and spiritualization. But nowhere, either for Greek or for Jew, was belief in the future life vivid, immediate, central and triumphant. Nowhere did the belief combine a conscious nearness of the world to come with a moral exalting of life in this present world. This was what Christianity brought. Its doctrine was not a flight to another world that left this world behind, nor was it a longing for another world that would come when the history of this world was ended. It was the very near certainty of another world, with which the Christians were already linked and into which the life of this world would be raised up.

For the Christian belief about the future state centred in Jesus Christ. He had been seen and loved in this life; and He had been seen and loved also as one who had conquered death. He had become vividly known as the Lord both of the living and of the dead; and the conviction of His people concerning the future life rested upon their conviction about Him in whose life they shared. It was an intense and triumphant conviction that where He was there also would His people be. It found utterance in ringing words. " He hath brought life and immortality to light through the Gospel." " Fear not; I am the first and the last, and the living one; and I was dead, and behold I am alive for evermore, and I have the keys of death and of Hades." " Awake, thou that sleepest and arise from the dead, and Christ shall shine upon thee."

Concerning the character of the life to come our Lord Himself says little. He reveals the God who rules that life and is Himself its centre, for it is a life unto God. It is not by speculations or by detailed revelation that men may win an understanding of the future state, but by conformity to the God who rules it and by knowledge of Jesus Christ who is the way to it. For He is not only the way to it, but Himself the very life of those who enter it. The central fact about the life of the Resurrection is that it is " in Christ." Some will share in that life by conscious faith in Christ, unless they betray that faith through their own lives. Others who have never known Him may share in it if, after the Parable of the Sheep and Goats, they have unconsciously ministered to Him. " In Christ "—whether by conscious faith or by a relationship that is at first unconscious—men shall be made alive.

Yet there is some explicit teaching concerning the nature of the Resurrection. By one dialogue and by one act Jesus Christ revealed that twofold aspect of the life to come which was to be summed up in the words "the Resurrection of the Body."

(1) Questioned by the Sadducees as to a point of casuistry concerning domestic relationships and their counterpart in the Resurrection, Jesus said that in the Resurrection " they neither marry nor are given in marriage; but are as angels in heaven " (Mark xii. 25). He said in effect that the Jewish beliefs which imported the conditions of this life into the Resurrection were wrong. The dead are transformed, so as to be like angels with bodies like " garments of light and glory." He added that the ground of belief in the future life is seen in the Scriptures, where God is the God of the dead patriarchs : they live because they belong to God who is " not the God of the dead but of the living."

(2) But thought the future life is to be a life transformed far beyond imagination and far beyond flesh and blood, men are indeed *raised*. " As touching the dead that they are raised " says Jesus. There is identity and continuity. And this is shewn in the act of the Lord's own Resurrection. While there was the glorifying of His body to which the narratives testify, there was also the continuity of the whole manhood, body and spirit, raised from death. The Son of God took

upon Him the whole of human nature (often in the New Testament the word "flesh" is so used) in order that the whole might be raised in glory.

II

Nothing is more impressive in the Apostolic writers than their refusal to exclude the body from its relevance to the moral issues of their faith and from the final destiny of the Christians. The Hellenistic environment of the Church almost cried out to it to assert a "spiritual" salvation, whereby men might escape from the prison of the body into a destiny from which all the transitory things of physical nature were excluded. But the Christians clung to the belief that the body had been divinely created and divinely redeemed. "Waiting for the adoption, to wit the redemption of our body": nothing less than that was their longing. They yearned "not to be unclothed, but clothed upon, that mortality might be swallowed up of life" (2 Cor. v. 4).

It is Paul who gives the most incisive expression to this belief. Food and digestion may belong to this earth, but the body belongs to Christ.

"Meats for the belly, and the belly for meats; but God shall bring to nought both it and them. But the body is not for fornication, but for the Lord: and the Lord for the body; and God both raised the Lord, and will raise up us through his power." (1 Cor. vi. 13-14.)

The body has its place in the great design of redemption through the Resurrection of Christ.

"If Christ is in you, the body is dead because of sin: but the spirit is life because of righteousness. But if the Spirit of him that raised up Jesus from the dead dwelleth in you, he that raised up Christ Jesus from the dead shall quicken also your mortal bodies through his Spirit that dwelleth in you." (Rom. viii. 10-11.)

Paul here says that the body of a Christian is indeed still liable to death owing to his share in the sinful race. But the essential being (" spirit " seems here so used) of a Christian is made alive because it belongs to the new life of righteousness. Is this essential being however divorced from the body? No, because the Father who raised up Jesus will extend His lifegiving action to the bodies of the Christians through the indwelling Spirit. The work of the Spirit in us prepares our bodies for the day when the Resurrection will accomplish in them all that God intends.

This consummation will be brought about at the Lord's return.

" For our citizenship is in heaven; from whence also we wait for a Saviour, the Lord Jesus Christ : who shall fashion anew the body of our humiliation, that it may be conformed to the body of his glory, according to the working whereby he is able even to subject all things unto himself." (Phil. iii. 20-21.)

It is possible that when he says " the body of his glory " Paul is thinking of the exalted Jesus whom he saw at his conversion, whence the words " glory " and " light " came to have for him a special meaning (cf. " the glory of God in the face of Jesus Christ," 2 Cor. iv. 6).

It is however in the fifteenth chapter of 1 Corinthians that the grand exposition of the doctrine occurs. Paul is here dealing with a crisis in the faith of some of his converts in Corinth. They are denying the Resurrection of the dead. Paul recalls his own teaching concerning the Resurrection of Christ, which the Corinthians had accepted. How impossible is their position now : for if Christians who have died do not rise again, then Christ cannot have been raised; the preaching of the Apostles has been worthless; the Christians must still be living in sin like the heathen, for it was the Resurrection of Christ alone that set them free. By denying the resurrection of the Christians they are denying the fact and the efficacy of the Resurrection of Christ. " But now hath Christ been raised from the dead, the firstfruits of them that are asleep. For since by man came death, by man came also the resurrection of the dead. For as in Adam all die, so also in Christ shall all be made alive " (xv. 20-22). The Resurrection of Christ is the prelude to the resurrection of the Christians. Whether Paul is here teaching a universal resurrection is not certain, for the concluding words just quoted are perhaps rightly taken by Moffatt as meaning " all the members of the Christian community." No safe conclusion can here be drawn concerning the question of universalism; Paul is asserting that the Resurrection is the beginning of a new order of life in which men may share : " Christ the firstfruits; then they that are Christ's at his coming " (xv. 23).

But how are the dead raised? and with what manner of body do they come? This is the crucial question for the Corinthians, and for all who are puzzled by the Gospel. Paul's answer (xv. 36-49) may thus be paraphrased. He points his readers to an analogy from nature. " Fool, do you not realize that in the everyday processes of the cornfield, there is an illustration of the secret about the Resurrection? You sow a seed; and you reap not a seed but something utterly unlike it yet truly derived from it, for the variety of forms and bodies in God's universe is quite limitless. Here then is your analogy for the Resurrection of the dead. The body comes into the world (this, rather than the burial of a corpse, seems to be the meaning of ' it is sown ') liable to death, and it is raised immortal :

> what is sown is mortal,
>   what rises is immortal :
> sown inglorious,
>   it rises in glory :
> sown in weakness,
>   it rises in power :
> sown an animate body,
>   it rises a spiritual body.

Adam was merely one into whom the breath of life had been breathed by God : Christ is one who Himself bestows life on others. Adam belonged to earth and to earth's limitations : Christ is heavenly, and comes from heaven. We have already experienced the life that is akin to the earthly Adam; and we are going to experience the life that is akin to the heavenly Christ."

Thus Paul tries to explain how the dead are raised. At this point he passes from the dead and speaks of "us" who will still be alive at the Parousia. "We shall not all sleep: i.e., we shall not all die; but we shall all be changed," transformed into the new and glorious life of the body when this "mortal shall have put on immortality." But it is with the dead that Paul's discussion is chiefly concerned, though no doubt they would be a minority. By the help of the analogy from nature he has affirmed a double truth. (1) The resurrection body will be utterly unlike the present body: indeed he says that "flesh and blood cannot inherit the kingdom of heaven." It is hard to imagine Paul ascribing to the risen body such actions as the eating of a piece of broiled fish. (2) Yet there is continuity. "Sown an animate body, it rises a spiritual body," or, as may be more correct: "there is sown an animate body, there rises a spiritual body." There is identity, as between seed and corn. It is a false inference, drawn by some, that the words "it is sown in corruption" mean that Christ's body perished in the grave and that the resurrection body is entirely new and unrelated to the past, for "it is sown" seems to refer not to burial but to the entry of the body into its existence in this world.

The analogy used by Paul serves to help his exposition: but it has its limits. Paul employs it for what it was worth; but he is equally insistent that the Resurrection involves a transcendental action of God which outruns human analogies and human understanding. "God giveth . . . as he wills." "I tell you a mystery." "Thanks be to God which giveth us the victory." It was less by the reasoned deductions from the analogy of nature than by belief in God's own unimaginable action that Paul's doctrine came into being; and its ground and its credibility rest upon the fact that Jesus Christ, the firstfruits, died and was buried and was raised and glorified. Similarly when Paul writes of a "spiritual body" the contrast is not between a body "formed out of matter" and a body "formed out of spirit"; it is between a body as we know it now and a body that has become the perfect instrument of the Holy Spirit, between a body that is conditioned by our present limitations and a body wherein the victory of Christ has done its perfect work. Some words of the late Fr. P. N. Waggett, S.S.J.E., may be quoted :

" The resurrection of the body may sometimes be called the ' physical resurrection,' but the phrase is likely to discredit the fact it points to. The Resurrection is a victory of spirit in the region where death now rules. We are not asked to believe in a reconstruction of the body after the fashion which belongs to the reign of death, but to believe that the death of the body as well as that of the spirit meets its conqueror in Christ. The death as we see is a real event, as real on its lower level of importance as the sin which is its counterpart in the spirit. And this real event of death, so serious, so tyrannous, so much unworthy to be the conclusion of the body's story, finds its cure in Christ. This cure lies in the victory of Christ over bodily death in His own person, and will be accomplished in His members by the extension of the same victory. ' God both raised the Lord, and will raise us through His power.' " (Paper on *The Resurrection* in *The Holy Eucharist with other occasional papers*, p. 199.)

It is believed by some scholars that in 2 Corinthians v. Paul shews an altered view, and has abandoned the doctrine of 1 Corinthians xv. in favour of a belief that is virtually the same as a Hellenistic doctrine of the immortality of the soul. This would imply an abandonment of the identity insisted upon in the former Epistle, and would be consistent with the decay of the body of Jesus in the tomb and the endowment of His spirit with a new body rather than the glorifying of the old. The discussion of the passage involves a lengthy treatment of exegetical problems; and rather than embark upon it here, the writer would refer his readers to the most recent examinations of the question, and would state the conclusions to which he himself has been led. These are : that in 2 Corinthians v. 2-4 Paul refers not to the fate of those who have died but to the fate of those who will be alive at the Parousia : that when the passage *is* so read the resemblances to 1 Corinthians xv. are impressive; that the argument for variations in Paul's belief has been unwarrantably exaggerated. The belief in the Resurrection of the body is, at a later date, found forcibly expressed both in Romans and in Philippians, which belie the notion that Paul abandoned his belief.[1]

The belief involves a far-reaching insight into the implications of the Gospel. Paul refuses to acquiesce in a contemporary Jewish conception of a resurrection after the pattern of carnal life as we know it. He equally refuses to succumb to a rigid divorce between spirit and matter, soul and body. He will not limit the word " body " to the body as we know it. Perhaps his familiarity with the phrase " the Body of Christ," which bore various meanings and yet expressed a personal identity, prepared him to feel his way towards a belief that the continuity of a body lies in its continuous relation to a person rather than in an identity of material particles. Be that as it may, his doctrine reaches far beyond the cleverness of the human mind or the pattern of human analogies: its source is in the Apostle's belief in God who created and redeemed both mankind and the material world, and in the event of the Gospel whereby Jesus Christ died and was buried and was raised again on the third day.

III

The interpretation of Paul's doctrine in subsequent Christian thought forms a rather complicated chapter in history. As in Judaism there were those who thought of the Resurrection of the dead in terms of the body as we know it in this world, and those who emphasized its transformation; so in the Christian Church there have been those who taught the Resurrection with the crudity that Paul deliberately avoided, and those who have entered into Paul's own insight. But it would be too simple to say merely that one school was right

[1] W. L. Knox on *S. Paul and the Church of the Gentiles*, pp. 135-145, argues that 2 Cor. v. 1-10 marks a change in Paul's belief under the influence of Hellenistic thought. But the similarity of belief in 1 Cor. xv. and 2 Cor. v 1-10 is convincingly shewn by L. S. Thornton in *The Common Life in the Body of Christ*, pp. 284-286.

and the other wrong. Those who adhered to a " crude " view
were sometimes bearing witness to a Christian view of the
body as against a " spirituality " which threatened the whole
Christian conception of man and the world. Already before
the first century was out there were those who insisted that,
alike in His earthly ministry and in His Resurrection, Christ
was merely a phantom; and against such teaching we find
Ignatius of Antioch (c. 112) insisting that, in both stages,
Christ was both spirit and flesh. In the second century,
Gnostics sought to tear Christianity from its historical roots,
to divorce the God who is spirit from the God who created
the material world, and to present Jesus Christ as one who
redeems us from matter and flesh as from evil things. It was
in face of these dangers that Christians asserted their belief
in the Resurrection of the flesh or of the body.

As regard the Creeds the main facts are as follows. The
western baptismal creeds, including the Apostles' Creed,
almost without exception professed belief in the *Resurrection
of the flesh*. This also appears in some early Eastern creeds,
such as the Creed of Jerusalem as given by S. Cyril. But
from the middle of the fourth century the prevailing form in
the East was the *Resurrection of the dead*. This was the form
that found its way into the longer " Nicene " Creed, and thus
became the authorized doctrine of the Universal Church. The
phrase is Scriptural, and it avoids the possibility of a crude
interpretation more readily than does the phrase " resurrection
of the flesh." In the Church of England at the Reformation
the " Nicene " Creed remained : " I look for the Resurrection
of the dead." As to the Apostles' Creed, in the form used
at Morning and Evening Prayer the word " flesh " was
altered by Cranmer into " body," but in the form used in Holy
Baptism the original phrase " resurrection of the flesh " was
retained.

(1) What has been called the " cruder " belief comes first
into view. The phrase " Resurrection of the flesh " was
apparently known in Rome before the end of the first century
(cf. Clement, 1 Cor. xxvi. 3). It was unscriptural. It could
easily be used to imply a conception far removed from that
of Paul, and it was in fact often so used. An instance often
cited is that of Tertullian who insisted that no part of the

present consituents of the body will be lost in the Resurrection, "not even a hair or an eye or a tooth." Had not Christ said that all the hairs of our head are numbered? "The flesh will arise, itself whole and entire" (*resurget caro, et quidem omnis, et quidem ipsa, et quidem integra*). In fairness to Tertullian it should be said that some of his other teaching greatly mitigates the crudity of these words; and the motive that prompted this teaching must be understood. But crudity there was, here and in other Latin writers; and there ensued, both within the Latin Church and subsequently within the Reformation Confessions, a presentation of the Resurrection which so interpreted the continuity of the body as to miss that view of the continuity which Paul had taught. For centuries many Christians have had a mental picture of the material particles of dead bodies being reassembled, and of the bodies rising from their graves at the last day. But this is a belief which the Creed does not compel and which Paul's teaching does not encourage.

(2) On the other hand there was another tradition. The phrase "Resurrection of the flesh" did not necessarily involve a crude belief. For in Biblical Greek the word "flesh" often bore the meaning, unknown in classical Greek, of "human nature" (cf. "all flesh shall see the salvation of God," "the Word was made flesh"). But this Biblical meaning was not always nor indeed more often, intended; and it was probably the crude possibilities of the word "flesh" that led Eastern Christians to prefer the expressions "Resurrection of the body" and "Resurrection of the dead." This brings us to the great teachers who insisted that the body in its true meaning cannot be understood in terms of its contemporary component particles.

The greatest teacher of this kind was Origen, the Alexandrine scholar of the third century. He held that the matter by which bodies exist is characterised by constant mutation. Wood is turned into fire, fire into smoke, smoke into air; a human body is like a river, for as the water departs and the river remains, so the particles composing a body depart and the body remains. In the Resurrection there will not be the solidity of the flesh, the liquid blood, the sinews, the structure of the limbs : yet the body will be there. Here we see with eyes, hear with ears and act with our hands. There "we shall be all sight, all hearing and all activity." "A certain principle lies within the body, from which, since it perishes not, the body is raised up in incorruption."

There is a modern ring in Origen's teaching. Westcott wrote of it: "There is no point in which his insight is more conspicuous; by keeping strictly to the Apostolic language he anticipated results which we have hardly yet secured. He saw that it is the spirit which moulds the frame through which it is manifested; that the body is the same not by any material continuity, but by the permanence of that which gives the law, the 'ratio,' he calls it, of its constitution. No exigencies of controversy, it must be remembered, brought Origen to his conclusion. It was, in his judgment, the clear teaching of S. Paul." Origen's view never died out. Though he was bitterly attacked by Jerome, his belief was in accord with "the resurrection of the dead" as the Nicene faith was to affirm it. In the ancient Church his teaching had some great adherents, including Chrysostom in his commentaries and Gregory of Nyssa in his *Soul and Resurrection*. In the modern era no disciple of Origen has been more ardent than Westcott himself, who links both Paul and Origen with those modern tendencies in thought which they anticipated.

For in truth the trend of modern science and philosophy seems to have features which confirm the credibility of the Pauline doctrine. The thought of a few decades ago was sometimes marked by a rigid contrast between spirit and matter, between personality and physical organism; and there are theologians who still hail this thought as if it were the last word of modernity. But to-day there is in physics the tendency to regard material objects as the organization of energy in particular forms, and to hold that the persistence of a body lies not in the immutability of its physical constituents but in their continued organization in accordance with the principle of the body's self-identity. Again, in the study of personality there is a reluctance to exclude the body from the essential self; in every act of consciousness the body plays its part as well as the mind. It is no doubt possible to shew that the mind may continue without the body, but it is impossible to conceive of a true life of the self without bodily expression. Indeed, the outlook of modern thought gives no encouragement to a sharp distinction between spirit and matter or to a belief in a spiritual life that can be diametrically contrasted with the bodily life. Rather does it seem to encourage us to beware of setting limits to the possibility of a bodily life that is both continuous and yet utterly different.

For science and theology concur in reminding us that our present experience of a body cannot set the limits to what a body may be. The New Testament speaks of the fleshly presence of Christ on earth as His body, of the Church as His body, and of the Eucharistic gift as His body. These phrases do not imply identity of material; but they are more than metaphors, and they tell of a true identity in that each is the organ of Christ's own activity. It is indeed only thus that the continuous identity of *any* body can rightly be defined. In the case of the body of the Resurrection, what eludes our knowledge and understanding is the manner of the transition between the present and the future states. Moreover there is this further point : the body here and the body hereafter are related not only to the self of the individual Christian, but also to the Christ to whom the Christian is united and in whose life the Christian will truly share. The relation between ourselves and *His* risen Body may be closer than we can imagine, for it is in *His* risen and glorious Body that we ourselves shall be made complete.

To abandon the use of the word " body " in connection with the Resurrection of the dead would indeed remove certain difficulties. But it would introduce difficulties no less great, and it would involve us in the poverty and materialism of limiting the word " body " to the body as we know it in its earthly and frustrated state. To cling to the words " the Resurrection of the body " is to affirm that in our present bodies there is the law of a bodily life beyond our dreams, when the Spirit of Him who raised up Jesus Christ has done His perfect work in us.

IV

The rejected stone may yet become the headstone of the corner. For it sums up the Christian view of the world. As Niebuhr said in the Gifford Lectures for 1939 it "embodies the very genius of the Christian idea of the historical" (*The Nature and Destiny of Man,* vol. ii., p. 305).

Man, nature and history have their solution not within themselves but within a divine kingdom that transcends them. This divine kingdom cannot be realized as a climax of human progress upon the plane of history, nor yet as a movement of mankind to an immortality that belongs to it by right. It will be realized by God's act in "raising up" mankind and delivering it from the contradictions which neither history nor immortality can solve. Yet this divine kingdom will not be far removed from nature and history; for in it both nature and history will be "clothed upon" and fulfilled.

> "Non eripit mortalia,
> Qui regna dat caelestia."

It is thus in the Resurrection of the dead that the goal of the individual and the goal of the redeemed society find their perfect coincidence. The individual cannot reach his goal except in union with those who shall share with Him in the love of God and in the Body of Christ. The traditional picture of a final Resurrection and of spirits waiting (though in a conscious and growing activity) for their bodies at the last day, tells of the truth that the perfecting of the individual is reached only in the perfecting of all. Thus the thought of my resurrection is inseparable from the thought of the resurrection of all the members of Christ.

The Resurrection of the body is something which the mind of man cannot conceive, just as the mind of man cannot conceive a purely spiritual immortality. But whereas a bodiless immortality is inconceivable because it seems to make the future life maimed and meaningless, the Resurrection of the body is inconceivable because it suggests a richness of life, in the blending of old and new, that defies human thought. The insight of a Paul, an Origen or a Westcott may assist our belief, and the analogies that lie near at hand may shew the rationality of the belief; but the point is soon reached when the Apostolic words confront us, " Behold I tell you a mystery. . . . Death is swallowed up in victory."

But the mystery springs from the infinite love of God, the creator and redeemer of mankind and of the world. Because His love is infinite it hath not entered into the heart of man to conceive the good things that He has prepared for them that love Him. But, because He is creator as well as redeemer, those good things will be fashioned not only from what is new but also from what is old. Nature will not be discarded, in order that men's souls alone may be salvaged and saved. The life of nature here and the life of the body which links us to nature will not be as a ladder, whereon we may climb to heaven and fling it aside when the ascent is finished. Rather will all that God has made have its place and its counterpart in the new heaven and the new earth. " Immortality " will be put on; but " this mortal " will find there its clothing and its home.

CHAPTER IX

Conclusion

I

" To learn the meaning of the Resurrection," wrote Westcott, " is the task not of one age only but of all." Just as the evangelists apprehended and presented different aspects of its meaning, so have the various epochs in the history of the Christian Church. There has yet to be written a great book telling of what the Resurrection has meant in the thought, doctrine and worship of Christians down the ages.

It was the news of Jesus and the Resurrection that first won the ancient world. In the Church of the Fathers it was specially the East that held the Resurrection in its central place. The Greek theologians seldom isolated the Cross; and the atonement meant to them the victory of the Resurrection, whereby nature rejoices in a new creation and whereby mankind may share in the risen life of Christ and so become partakers of the divine nature. Similarly the worship of the Eastern Church has clung to the Resurrection in a way that the West, both Latin and Reformed, has strangely missed. For if in the West we are wont to think of ourselves as worshipping upon earth and of Christ coming down to us in the Eucharist, the East has never forgotten that the bread and the wine and the worshippers and earth itself are lifted up to heaven where Christ is. To attend the liturgy of the Eastern Church is to perceive and to feel how far the West has missed the realization that the first truth in Christian worship is that as Christians we have been raised together in the heavenly places with Christ.

It would be absurd to say that the West lost sight of the Resurrection, for every saintly life and every achievement of Christian thinking bears witness to it. Yet there have been phases in the West when the Cross was isolated and seen without the light of Easter upon it. The tendency can be traced in art, where the crucifix with the figure of the dead Christ upon it replaced the earlier " Majestas " crucifix with Christ crowned, robed and victorious. It can be traced in doctrine, where the sacrifice of the atoning death has often been separated from the victory of the atoning Resurrection. It can be traced in worship, where the commemoration of Calvary in the liturgy has replaced the commemoration of the whole drama of God's redemption. In all this, sweeping generalizations are out of place. It is often inevitable for Christians to fix their gaze solely upon " Jesus Christ and Him crucified," to know nothing save the Cross; and when they do so they are indeed near to the Resurrection. None the less there has sometimes been a concentration upon the Cross that is less than Pauline, and there is a germ of truth in Westcott's words: " It has been indeed disastrous for our whole view of the Gospel that a late age placed upon the Cross the figure of the dead Christ, and that we have retained it there " (*Revelation of the Risen Lord,* p. 27).

To-day we have behind us a century in which there has

been teaching upon the Resurrection as great as any in the long centuries since the Apostolic Age. In England two great teachers made it their central theme. One was Richard Meux Benson, of Cowley, who penetrates farther than perhaps any other writer into the necessity of seeing the Passion with the light of Easter upon it and of understanding the Resurrection only in terms of faith in the Crucified. "How entirely the Passion is seen simply through the lustrous halo of the Resurrection in S. Paul" (*Spiritual Letters*, p. 54). "Our victory can only be the victory of the dead" (*ibid.*, p. 115).

The other was Westcott. The more it has seemed that some of the tendencies since his day have proved onesided and unfruitful, the more does the greatness of his work stand out. His theme was the place of the Resurrection as the climax of creation no less than of redemption. With his thinking moulded by the study of the Johannine writings Westcott presented the Resurrection both as the fulfilment of the processes of nature and history and as the miraculous entrance of a new divine order into both. On the one hand "We see in the risen Christ the end for which man was made, and the assurance that the end is within reach. The Resurrection, if we may so speak, shews us the change which would have passed over the earthly life of man, if sin had not brought in death" (*Revelation of the Risen Lord*, p. xxxiv.). On the other hand "There was a tendency towards the central truth of history but there was no tendency to produce it" (*Gospel of the Resurrection*, p. 72). "It is either a miracle or an illusion. . . . It claims to be the opening of a new life to the world. It cannot then be rightly contemplated by comparing it with the events of common history" (*ibid.*, p. 52). Both the historical and the transcendental, both the humanism of the Gospel and its supernatural character, are authenticated by the Resurrection. "Paganism proclaims the grandeur of man : Judaism the supremacy of God. Christianity accepts the antithesis and vindicates by the message of the Resurrection the grandeur of man in and through God" (*ibid.*, p. 210).

II

The years that have passed since Westcott wrote those words have seen the most violent movements in events and in theology. In events there has been the great expansion of humane and scientific progress, and subsequently the catastrophe of two great wars. In theology there has been first the heyday of the liberal school, and subsequently the rediscovery of the supernatural and transcendental aspects of the Biblical revelation.

The liberal movement in theology advanced very sure of itself. It had roots in some of the great Christian affirmations, and a kinship with the Christian humanism both of Alexandria and of the Renaissance. It knew that the world was made by God, and that in Him was life, and the life was the light of men. It was able to shew how the processes of evolution in nature and of history in man were a gradual unfolding of the Spirit of God the Creator. It related creation with evolution, revelation with historical development. God is present in time and in change, as the created world with man as its crown struggles forward towards its goal.

But in the latter days of liberal theology it became increasingly apparent that a great omission was being made. Over-zealous in its alliance with contemporary ideas of progress and contemporary hopes of a divine kingdom to be realized by a steady growth within history, liberal theology neglected the truths that God is transcendent and that His supreme revelation is an intervention from above and the beginning of a new creation. Hence it was easy to present the Resurrection as the disclosure of the hope of mankind's ascent to God through a spiritual immortality. It was less easy to grasp that it is the victory of God over sin and death. The event that is the supreme symbol of the transcendence of the living God was turned into a symbol of His presence within the advance of humanity, and little more.

It was in reaction from liberal theology that Karl Barth and his school uttered afresh the message of God's otherness and sovereignty and His mighty act in the Resurrection, as the

war of 1914-1918 was drawing to its close. The Resurrection
was central in the message of Barth; and he recalled Christians
whose minds were full of man's religion, man's experiences
and man's progress, to the Act of the living God which confronts a race helpless to save itself. *" Jesus Christ our Lord.
This is the Gospel and the meaning of history. In this name
two worlds meet, two planes intersect, the one known and
the other unknown. . . . Jesus has been declared to be the
Son of God with power according to the Holy Spirit through
His resurrection from the dead.* In this declaration and ap-
pointment—which are beyond historical definition—lies the
true significance of Jesus. Jesus as the Christ, as the Messiah,
is the End of History; and He can be comprehended only as a
Paradox, as Victory, as Primal History. . . . The Resurrection
is the revelation; the disclosing of Jesus as the Christ; the
appearing of God; the apprehending of God in Jesus. . . . In
the Resurrection the new world of the Holy Spirit touches the
old world of the flesh, but touches it as a tangent touches a
circle, that is, without touching it " (Barth, *Epistle to the
Romans,* Eng. trans., pp. 29-30). It may be hard to assent
to all Barth's propositions, but it is harder still to deny that
he has stirred Christians in every land and tradition to face
once more the transcendental and catastrophic themes of the
New Testament.

In the recent trends in Biblical theology it is the treatment
of history that is often somewhat questionable. It is rightly
said that the Resurrection is more than a historical event, and
that it is is impossible to demonstrate it by evidential proofs
apart from faith in God. We are rightly reminded that the
empty tomb of itself was not and could never be the cause
of Christian belief in the Resurrection. But sometimes
Biblical theologians appear to deny that the examination of
historical evidence had in the Apostolic age, and can have
to-day, *any* part in the Resurrection faith (cf. Brunner, *The
Mediator,* pp. 573-579). Here it is hard to follow. It seems
utterly true that the Resurrection " is as invisible, as unthink-
able, as the Incarnation " (*ibid.,* p. 573), that " Easter is not
an historical event to be reported," that " the Apostles' witness is based upon the fact that they received a revelation ";

we can agree, and be grateful for the reminder. But does it follow that the evidence, including that of the empty tomb, had no place at all? Rather than accept this paradoxical treatment both of history and of the place of reason in the receiving of revelation, it seems wiser to draw back and to attempt the harder task of holding together both the serious treatment of historical evidence and the belief in the living God of the Bible. Is it possible to learn from the shaking that Barth has given to us, and yet to return and to use what Westcott had taught us?

III

It is the message of the Bible, in all its richness, that the people of our generation need. It is insufficient and misleading to present the Old Testament as the story of the growth of mans' ideas about God, without the primacy of the greater theme of God's own acts and God's own utterances in the events of Israel's history that makes the Old Testament what it is. It is equally misleading to present the Gospel as the conception of God taught by Jesus, without due reference to the mighty act of God Himself in the Passion and the Resurrection. Read in its own light, the Bible has the Resurrection as its key. Its God is the God who raised up Jesus Christ from the dead, and in so doing vindicated His word in the Old Testament and in the Cross of Christ. It is only in virture of the Resurrection that the Bible is one, and that the message of the Bible is coherent and true.

But though the revelation in the Bible is unique and breaks into the world from above, it is not " wholly other." For the God who there reveals Himself is also the God who created the world. Therefore the theme of the Gospel, Life-through-Death, does not come as wholly strange to the world. Rather is it like a pattern already woven into nature and into the life of man. Though it is blurred by human sinfulness the pattern is not obliterated; and throughout all life there runs, however faintly perceived, a law of living through dying, a law whose presence testifies that man is made in the image of God. The Gospel of the glory of God in the face of Jesus Christ is both strange to mankind and yet nearer to mankind than the breath which they breathe. For the truth in Him is also the truth in them:

> *Und so lang Du das nicht hast*
> *Dieses-Stirb und Werde*
> *Bist Du nur ein trueber Gast*
> *Auf dieser dunklen Erde.*

Note (A): *The Ascension*

THE Creeds distinguish two separate events, the Resurrection and the Ascension. In so far as it is only Luke who describes the latter event Christian tradition derives its conception of the event from Luke's narratives. In Luke xxiv. 50-52 Jesus blessed the disciples " and was parted from them." The words " and was carried up into heaven " are textually doubtful, and it cannot be affirmed with certainty that the " Ascension " is mentioned in these verses. But in Acts i. 9, the reference to the Ascension is clear; at the close of forty days Jesus "was taken up and a cloud received him from out of their sight." The narrative has resemblances to the story of the ascension of Elijah. Besides this narrative, there are in the New Testament many references to Jesus " going to heaven " or " being exalted " or passing " to the right hand of God " or " ascending." It is generally believed that these phrases refer to an event distinct from the Resurrection and identical with that described in Acts i. 9.

It is possible however that the Apostolic writers often made little or no separation between the Resurrection and the exaltation to heaven, and that where a distinction is made it may be due in part to the existence of two kinds of imagery: (1) the raising of Jesus from death, (2) the entrance of Jesus into the heavenly Lordship foretold in Psalm cx. Jesus was no longer among the dead, for God had raised Him. Jesus was no longer sharing in the limitations of His earthly life, for all sovereignty in heaven now was His. Both facts may be embraced in the confession " Jesus is Lord "; and both facts,

with no clear division between them may be included in such
references to the glorifying of Jesus as Rom. viii. 34, Phil. ii.
9, Col. iii. 1, Eph. i. 20, 1 Tim. iii. 16, Acts ii. 33, 1 Peter i.
21, iii. 21-22.

Yet the tradition in Luke concerning the Ascension as a
distinct event cannot be dismissed. There is nothing incredible
in an event whereby Jesus assured the disciples that the
appearances were ended and that His sovereignty and His
presence must henceforth be sought in new ways. It
is true that the Apostles believed in a three-storeyed
universe, and would think of the exaltation of Jesus as a
journey through the skies to a local heaven. Yet the abandonment of their astronomy does not involve the modification of
their essential doctrine; for more than one passage in the New
Testament makes it clear that they realized that the exaltation
of Jesus implied a sovereignty and an omnipresence that
transcend astronomy altogether.

In an important essay, " Jesus the Lord," in the volume
entitled *Mysterium Christi* (1930) Dr. Hermann Sasse pointed
out that although the Resurrection and the Exaltation are
hardly to be separated as historical events they are to be
distinguished as theological truths. It was one thing to assert
that Jesus Christ was no longer held fast by death. It was
another thing to confess that He shares in the eternity, omnipresence and omnipotence of God. All this was implied in
the confession " Jesus is Lord," and only " in the Holy
Spirit " could the confession be made (cf. 1 Cor. xii. 3).

Note (B): *Appearance and Vision*

In his essay upon the Resurrection in *Essays Catholic and
Critical* (1926) Dr. E. G. Selwyn suggested that the appearances of the risen Lord may be regarded as visions akin to
those experienced by Christian mystics. His view is very
different from the vision theories discussed in Chapter IV of
this book, for he attaches the greatest importance to the event
of the Resurrection, attested by the empty tomb, before and
behind the appearances of the risen Lord. But he makes it

clear that, if we believe that the glorified Lord passed to a new and mysterious mode of existence, there may not be a great deal of difference between temporary accommodations to the former mode of existence (Westcott's view) and visions granted to the disciples. Whether Dr. Selwyn's own interpretation is convincing or not it is plainly congruous with the Gospel and the Creed. Indeed his discussion brings into very clear relief the distinctive importance of the two foundations—" He was raised " and " He appeared."

BIBLIOGRAPHY

Among older works specially worth reading are Bishop Westcott's *The Gospel of the Resurrection* and *The Revelation of the Risen Lord*. The most important work from the standpoint of a very radical criticism was Kirsopp Lake's *The Historical Evidence for the Resurrection of Jesus Christ*. A mass of information about different theories and interpretations can be found in W. J. Sparrow-Simpson's *The Resurrection and Modern Thought*.

The following list is of works more recent, and easily obtainable.

John Baillie. *The Life Everlasting* (shews the bearing of the Resurrection upon ideas about the life after death).

F. Morison. *Who moved the Stone?* (An exciting, if somewhat speculative discussion of what happened on the first Easter morning).

G. D. Yarnold. *Risen Indeed* (A study, both scientific and devotional, of the Resurrection narratives).

E. G. Selwyn. Essay entitled "The Evidence for the Resurrection" in *A New Commentary on Holy Scripture* (ed. Charles Gore); and essay entitled "The Resurrection in *Essays Catholic and critical*.

C. H. Dodd. Essay entitled "The Appearances of the Risen Christ: an essay in Form-Criticism of the Gospels," in the volume *Studies in the Gospels* edited by D. E. Nineham.

INDEX OF SUBJECTS

INDEX OF NAMES